Undergrounding Electric Lines

Anthony J. Pansini, E.E., P.E.

𝄃𝄃𝄃

HAYDEN BOOKS

A Division of Macmillan Computer Publishing

11711 North College, Carmel, Indiana 46032 USA

In Memory of
John De Lellis
Friend, Engineer, Exemplar

© 1978 by Hayden Books
A Division of Howard W. Sams & Co.

FIRST EDITION
NINTH PRINTING—1991

International Standard Book Number: 0-8104-0827-9
Library of Congress Catalog Card Number: 78-4447

Printed in the United States of America

Preface

The undergrounding of utility lines has been the subject of increasing attention in recent years, both by engineers who see this as a means of bettering service reliability at an acceptable incremental cost, and by the general public who view it additionally as a means of improving appearance. New developments in plastics and in construction methods have made possible the modernization of electrical utilities and further refinements will, no doubt, attest to the economics and desirability of undergrounding these facilities. Recognition of these developments by the utility companies is found in their expansion of such underground systems, and by many of the governmental agencies, who have legislated ordinances making such installations mandatory for the future in certain areas.

The text has been kept simple, and highly technical engineering procedures have been avoided; many illustrations help in the understanding of the problems involved and their solutions.

Grateful acknowledgment is made to the many manufacturers and suppliers for their contributions of illustrations, diagrams, and other descriptive material; to Mr. Arthur C. Seale, Jr., for his aid in the preparation of this work; to Mrs. Ruby Jane DeFoore for her stenographic assistance; to the staff of the Hayden Book Company; and, finally, to my family and friends for their encouragement and understanding.

ANTHONY J. PANSINI

Waco, Texas

Contents

1. **GENERAL CONSIDERATIONS** 1

*History • Electric Supply Systems • Overhead vs. Under-
ground • Underground Transmission • Underground
Urban Distribution • Underground Residential Distribution (URD) • Safety and Reliability • Economics •
Hazards • Trends*

   Review 11

   Study Questions 12

2. **PLANNING CONSIDERATIONS** 13

*Introduction • Transmission Systems • Distribution Lay-
outs: Primary Supply • Radial Systems • Open-Loop Systems • Closed-Loop Systems • Duplicate Supply Systems
• Secondary Network Systems • Primary Voltages • Distribution Layouts: Transformers, Secondary Mains, and
Services • Underground Construction*

   Review 22

   Study Questions 23

3. **DESIGN CONSIDERATIONS** 24

*Cables • Transmission Cables • Pressure-Type Cables •
Stop-Joints • Charging Currents • Distribution Cables
• Primary Cables • Secondary Cables • Splices • Transformers • Transformer Tanks • Grounds • Protective Devices • Ducts and Manholes*

   Review 46

   Study Questions 47

4. INSTALLATION CONSIDERATIONS 48

Trenching and Plowing • Duct and Manhole Installation • Transmission Systems • Distribution Systems • Manholes • Cable Installation • Transmission Cable • Buried Distribution Cable • Equipment Installation • Coordination of Utilities • Ducts and Manholes • Risers and Potheads • Safety

Review 70

Study Questions 71

5. MAINTENANCE AND OPERATION CONSIDERATIONS 73

Locating Underground Facilities • Excavation • Work on Cables • Transmission Cables • Secondary Distribution Cables • Work on Transformers and Equipment • Electrolysis • Restoration of Service • Radial Circuits • Duplicate Primary Supply • Closed-Loop Circuit • Open-Loop Circuit • Low Voltage Network • Fault Finding • Isolation of Faulted Section • Cable Locating • Fault Breakdown • Fault Location • Tracing Current • Capacitance Method • Traveling Wave • Wheatstone Bridge • Crude Method • Fault Indicators • Conclusions

Review 96

Study Questions 98

INDEX 99

Undergrounding
Electric Lines

general considerations

History

The first commercial delivery of electric energy was through an underground system, installed in New York City in 1882 by Thomas Edison. It consisted of heavy copper bars, surrounded by pitch, contained in fiber tubes, buried in the ground. The energy supplied was by direct current at a pressure of approximately 100 V. The high cost of this construction, together with the rapid loss in electric pressure as the distance from the generating plant increased, restricted the widespread development of the early electric supply systems.

The application of the transformer in 1886 in Great Barrington, Massachusetts, completely changed the character of such distribution systems. Direct current gave way to alternating current, and the electric pressures used climbed to about 1,000 V. But, perhaps, the most significant change was in the type of construction using small conductors installed overhead.

The transformer also made practical the bulk delivery of electric energy over long distances; for example, from a remotely located power plant to a distribution center. In the same year, 1886, ac power was delivered at 2,000 V over a 30-km overhead transmission line built at Cerchi, Italy. Continuing improvements in technology has made possible the transmission of ever-increasing amounts of electric energy over longer and longer distances at higher and higher voltages.

These more economical systems spread rapidly and made practical the supply of electricity, even to suburban and rural areas. Until the

Fig. 1-1 In the early 1900s the "sidewalks of New York" ran beneath a maze.

middle of the twentieth century, this was almost exclusively the method of supply in those areas. The profusion of overhead electric, telephone, and telegraph wires in the downtown areas of major cities made their installation underground economically and esthetically desirable (Fig. 1–1).

The many and varied uses of the plastic materials developed during and after World War II enabled the further extension of underground systems in urban as well as in suburban and rural areas.

Electric Supply Systems

Electricity is produced at generating stations and transmitted in bulk quantities over high-voltage transmission lines to substations, where it is subdivided into quantities at lower voltages supplying individual areas, and finally brought in smaller quantities at still lower

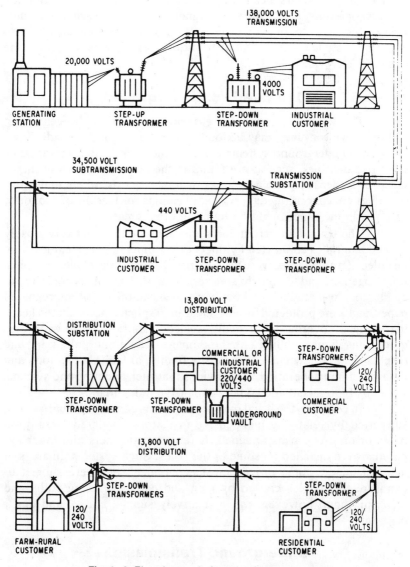

Fig. 1–2 Electric supply from generator to customer.

voltages into homes and industry. In our pictorial rendition, note that the generator produces electricity at a pressure of 20,000 V. This is raised, by a transformer, to 138,000 V (or higher) for the long transmission journey over lines to transmission substations located in important load areas of the territory. Here, it may be stepped down to 69,000 V (or lower) for transmission in smaller quantities to distribution substations. Each of these feeds its local load area by means of primary distribution feeders, operating at 13,800 V (or higher or lower). Distribution transformers connect to the primary voltage, which is stepped down to approximately 120 or 240 V for distribution over secondary mains to the customer's service (Fig. 1–2).

Overhead vs. Underground

The lines that carry this electric energy from the generating station to the consumer may be found overhead or underground. Originally, such underground systems were confined almost solely to areas of high load densities, such as are found in the downtown areas of major cities, or to densely populated areas such as may exist where multistory dwellings are concentrated; special applications for reasons of economy, safety, or appearance might be found in other areas.

The usual underground systems consisted of relatively closely spaced manholes connected by ducts or conduits in which cables were installed. The manholes were used to install and test the cables, to splice them together, and to contain some equipment. The cables consisted of conductors insulated with rubber, varnished cambric or oil-impregnated paper, and were protected by lead sheathing; splicing necessitated keeping the lead covering hermetically sealed. Failure in these cables required unsplicing, pulling out the damaged cable and pulling in, and resplicing, of a new cable. Often, the finding of faults was a long and time-consuming operation. It is obvious that such underground systems were costly to install and equally expensive to maintain.

In contrast, the usual overhead systems consisted of bare wires, supported by relatively inexpensive insulators, mounted directly on poles or on cross-arms attached thereto; transformers and other apparatus were installed on some of the poles. Such systems, in areas of lighter load densities, proved most economical, but were subject to exposure to troubles caused by man and nature. Finding faults and repairing them, however, was a relatively simple, cheap, and quick operation.

Underground Transmission

For a long time, the placing of transmission lines underground where there was a possible overhead route was thought unreasonable by utilities (both privately and publicly owned) and the general public. The relatively higher cost was generally accepted as sufficient reason for overhead by regulatory bodies as well as the public. Changing ideas for undergrounding of electric lines has made such underground installations—in whole, but mostly in part—more numerous; more transmission being placed underground because of esthetics, "environmental compatability and public need," regardless of economics.

In open areas (glide paths of runways in the vicinity of airports, for example) and in suburban areas where unpaved rights-of-way were not available, such transmission lines usually consisted of steel armored lead-sheathed cables buried directly in the ground. Through urban and paved city streets (to supply distribution substations in built-up areas, for example), lead-sheathed cables pulled into ducts (sometimes also referred to as trunk ducts, or trunks) installed between manholes spaced relatively far apart (typically 500 to 2,500 feet) was the usual method employed (Fig. 1–3).

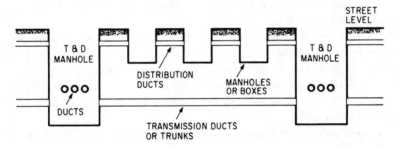

Fig. 1–3 Transmission and distribution duct system in urban and densely populated areas.

Operating voltage levels of underground cables in general were less than those of overhead transmission lines. It was often necessary, therefore, to step down overhead line voltages by means of transformers to accommodate the lower available levels of the underground cables, stepping them up again when the lines continued overhead.

Until the late 1920s, transmission cables generally consisted of so-called solid insulation, varnished cambric or oil-impregnated paper, wrapped around stranded copper conductors, the whole encased in a lead sheath. Such single-conductor cables were generally limited to circuits operating at a maximum of about 45 kV. More complex cables, employing oil or gas under pressure in association with their insulation, later permitted safe operation at voltage level of higher values approaching 500 kV; in some instances, when not lead-sheathed, they were encased in steel pipes. Recent developments of plastic insulation have replaced oil-impregnated paper and other insulations in cables rated up to

69 kV; plastics have also taken the place of lead in the sheaths (and eliminated armor in some instances). Such plastic-type cables have greatly simplified the handling and splicing of such cables at a greatly reduced cost.

Underground Urban Distribution

In urban areas where streets are generally paved and rear-lot rights-of-way are generally not available because of inaccessibility or usage of the area by the customer, cables pulled into ducts are almost exclusively employed in electric distribution systems. Manholes are spaced closer together to enable supply to buildings from services emanating from them, with duct runs consequently shorter in length.

Cables installed in them were generally of the solid-insulation type, using rubber, varnished cambric, and oil-impregnated paper, conductors of copper and sheaths made of lead. They were of the single-conductor or multiconductor type; the latter usually composed of two or three insulated conductors contained within a single sheath, for greater economy and ease in handling.

The distribution cables operated at two separate and distinct voltage levels: from about 2,000 to 15,000 V, called primary cables to distinguish them from those operating at lower values, usually 100 to 600 V, called secondary cables. Rubber insulation was generally restricted to the secondary cables and to some primary cables in the lower, approximately 2,000-V, range.

The advent of reliable and more economic plastics has made possible the replacement of the former insulations (at all the above voltage levels) and lead sheathing with those made of appropriate plastic compounds. This, together with the adoption of aluminum for the conductor in most applications, has made for less expensive cables more easily handled. Further economy and simplified construction resulted from the installation of ducts also made of plastic material.

Underground Residential Distribution (URD)

Higher standards of living, creating an increasing usage of electricity, brought about a demand for undergrounding electric lines in urban and suburban residential areas, not only to obtain greater reliability by decreasing their exposure to hazards, but to improve appearance as well. The development of plastics, not only for electric insulation, but as mechanical protective coverings, made it possible to achieve this desirable goal.

Conductors (aluminum or copper) insulated and protected by coatings of such plastics, buried (in excavations or plowed) directly in the ground, in long lengths (without ducts, manholes, lead sheaths, and difficult splices), so drastically reduced installation and maintenance costs, as to make the consideration of this type of underground system economically feasible to take the place of typical overhead systems.

The potential for further economy, through the simultaneous installation of the facilities of other utilities (telephone, CATV, gas, water, etc.), although creating other problems, also helps. Although the technical problems for such joint construction have been resolved, the administrative problems involved are formidable, but have been resolved (Fig. 1-4).

In the past, some direct burial installations of cables were made, employing armor wires over the usual lead sheath as protection; such armor may be dispensed with in present plastic-sheathed direct-buried cables.

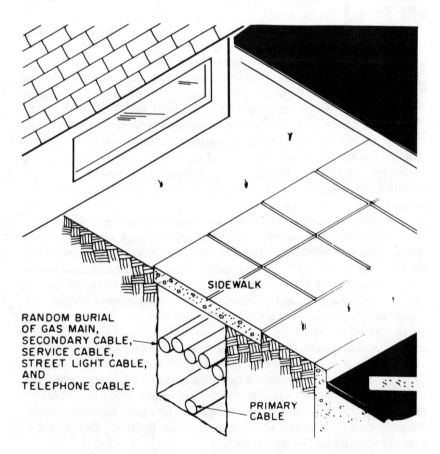

Fig. 1-4 Typical "joint" underground distribution system.

While such underground installations are now being made almost universally, existing overhead installations probably will not be replaced to any great extent, until other factors make them obsolete.

Safety and Reliability

The installation of electric facilities beneath the surface of the ground removes them from hazards associated with the actions of people and with the vicissitudes of nature, to which overhead lines are exposed. Direct contact with people, or people carrying objects (ladders, kites, rods, etc.), or indirectly through cars hitting poles, sagging or corroded conductors extending to or near the ground, wind, lightning, snow and ice, salt spray, and dirt all affect reliability of service; to these may be added birds, snakes, rodents, squirrels, insects, and even larger animals, making contact or causing equipment failures—all of which have occurred. Trees, growing into or near overhead lines, have been the cause of many faults, causing momentary or extended circuit interruptions; programs for tree trimming to control such situations, have been expensive and often the source of complaint.

On the other hand, buried conductors and facilities are subject to "dig-ins," accidental contacts from construction or other excavation, with no knowledge of the existence of the facilities; floods and earthquakes, corrosion and other chemical actions, and stray electric currents causing electrolytic action also impose the possibility of cable failure. Unlike overhead facilities, where failures may frequently be observed, the location of failures on underground facilities is not as readily known, and time-consuming methods are generally employed to locate and repair such failures.

On overhead systems, contamination and incipient faults, usually associated with insulators and mounting facilities, cause small and irregular or intermittent currents to leak to adjacent structures (and ground); these act as small radio transmitters, resulting in local radio, TV, and telephone interference. In general, this is obviated by the underground construction, although faulty underground cables can cause interference in adjacent telephone circuits.

The disappearance of utility facilities in the air obviously contributes to improving the general appearance and maintain property values in the community; while such facilities may have an esthetic appeal to some utility engineers, it is almost certain they do not affect the average layman in the same manner. Economics, however, tends to cause some acceptance of certain otherwise less than ideal conditions. Further, no longer need trees be trimmed, cut down, or otherwise disturbed to accommodate utility lines.

Economics

The installation of plastic-insulated and protected conductors, whether pulled into ducts or buried directly in the ground, by means outlined earlier, have greatly reduced the cost of such underground installations as compared to similar overhead facilities. In general, while this ratio is still in favor of overhead-type construction, it has dropped to a point where, with the greater emphasis placed on reliability and appearance, underground construction warrants serious consideration. Individual studies are necessary to determine comparative costs in individual areas and under particular circumstances.

Some additional saving is actually realized in the construction of overhead circuits. For economy and appearance, it is often preferable to use one pole for both electric power and communication lines; this is known as joint construction. Costs are shared by all the parties using the pole; these include not only the electric and telephone lines, but CATV, and on occasion, telegraph, fire alarm, and traffic control circuits, and other circuits (Fig. 1-5).

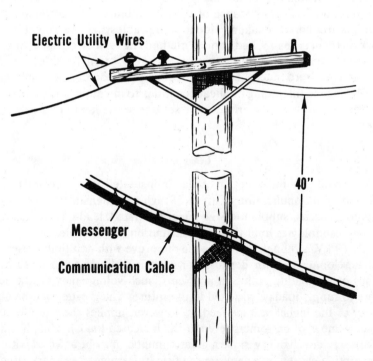

Fig. 1-5 Joint construction of telephone and electric cables.

Further economies are obviously possible, if the facilities of several utilities are installed simultaneously. Many of the problems involving the coordination of such efforts, from the planning stage to final construction, present administrative and logistical problems of such proportions that the solutions may very well reduce or wipe out the potential savings indicated.

Hazards

During construction and maintenance, such underground systems present unusual hazards to both the public and workers. Because they often require work, whether digging or plowing, on regularly traversed streets and much frequented areas, the hazards to bystanders from construction activities, cave-ins, and equipment operation require special precautions to overcome. Overhead work, on the other hand, may often be done in rear-lot areas, and above the ground, out of the general area hazardous to the public.

For the workers, the usual hazards attendant on construction work are present in both overhead and underground installations; however, once installed, extraordinary hazards arise in the maintenance of underground facilities because of their invisibility. Extraordinary precautions are therefore taken to identify the cables and equipment before work on them is begun, and various methods have been devised for such operations to prevent injury to workers. Very often facilities are de-energized and grounded before operations proceed; this not only adds to the expense (including duplicate facilities to maintain service in some cases), but may cause interference to service where facilities are deenergized.

Trends

While the introduction of plastic-insulated and protected cables has also found application in areas of high load densities, such as the downtown areas, supplanting the paper-insulated, lead-covered cables, present technologies limit these to distribution power cables of approximately 69 kV, although this value may improve with additional research and development. With demand for electricity likely to increase as a means of combating pollution problems, such voltage may not be adequate to supply loads envisioned in the future. The greater load-hauling ability of the higher voltage feeders, however, implies their supply to a larger number of customers (even at the increased loads). This, in turn, affects service reliability, since a greater number may be affected with an interruption caused by a fault on the feeder. Designs of primary circuits may, therefore, incorporate features for the rapid manual or automatic transfer of the unfaulted portion of the feeder to other sources, limiting the number of customers affected. This applies equally to both overhead and underground systems.

With expected further improvements in materials and methods, the expansion of underground to new electric systems appears likely. Not only should economics improve, but the continued pressure for improved service reliability and appearance, all tend to reinforce this trend. Conversion of existing overhead systems to underground, however, may be confined to special cases.

Review

- Electricity is produced at generating stations and transmitted in bulk quantities over high-voltage transmission lines to substations, where it is subdivided into quantities at lower voltages supplying individual areas, and finally brought in smaller quantities at still lower voltages into homes and industry (Fig. 1–2).
- The lines that carry this electric energy from the generating station to the consumer may be found overhead or underground. Safety, economy, appearance, or other special conditions often make underground construction desirable; the development of plastic materials has made practical the further adoption of underground systems.
- Underground cables consist of insulated conductors protected against damage during installation and from soil conditions and other underground hazards by a rugged and moisture-proof metallic or plastic sheath. In special instances, they may be further protected by steel wires spirally wound on the outside of the sheaths.
- In congested or commercial areas, cables are installed in ducts or conduits, usually made of concrete or transite, but may also be made of wood, plastic, fiber, and, where extra strength and rigidity are required, of steel. These ducts run between manholes spaced relatively far apart for transmission lines and closer together for distribution lines. The manholes are used to install or remove cables, to splice and test them, and to contain certain equipment.
- Operating voltage levels of underground cables, in general, are less than those of overhead transmission lines. It is often necessary, therefore, to step down overhead line voltages by means of transformers to accommodate the lower available levels of the underground cables, stepping them up again when the lines continue overhead.
- In residential and suburban areas, cables may be buried directly in the ground. For greater economy, they may be buried in the same trench with gas, telephone, CATV, water, and other utilities (Fig. 1–4).

- While the installation of electric facilities underground removes them from the hazards associated with actions of people and the vicissitudes of nature, they are subject to "dig-ins," accidental contacts during excavation, floods and earthquakes, corrosion and other chemical action, and from stray electric currents causing electrolytic action.
- Unlike overhead facilities, where failures may be frequently observed and readily repaired, the location of failures on underground facilities is not as readily known, and time-consuming and more elaborate methods are generally required to locate and repair such failures.

Study Questions

1. What are some advantages of underground electric systems? Disadvantages?
2. What are some advantages of overhead electric systems? Disadvantages?
3. What are the three main parts of an underground cable?
4. What are some of the materials used for insulation in underground cables?
5. What are the advantages of plastic insulations?
6. Why are underground cables sheathed? What materials are used?
7. What are the components of underground systems in areas of high load density?
8. What are advantages of buried underground systems? Disadvantages?
9. What has made practical the installation of underground electric systems in suburban and rural areas?
10. What is meant by joint construction?

2

planning considerations

Introduction

It cannot be sufficiently stressed that the advantages deriving from the lower exposure of underground installations (as compared to overhead) are offset somewhat by the difficulties in finding faults when they do occur, and the usually greater time required for their restoration. Hence, in order to maintain acceptable standards of service reliability, it may be necessary to adopt designs which, as a rule, are more costly, the degree of complexity (and cost) depending on the desired standard.

Transmission Systems

The function of transmission systems is to carry bulk loads from a power plant to load centers, between load centers, or between utility systems, all involving relatively great distances, since the terminals are usually rather remote from each other. Because of the importance of these principal sources of supply, duplicate (multiple) installation of facilities is often required, frequently from different sources and via separate alternate routes. Further, construction specifications provide for a high degree of operating reliability, not only to minimize periods of interruptions, but also to expedite restoration in event of fault.

Some typical layouts of transmission circuitry of varying complexity and degrees of reliability are shown in the accompanying diagrams (Fig. 2–1). In practice, each line can represent one or more separate feeders and the transmission system can consist of a combina-

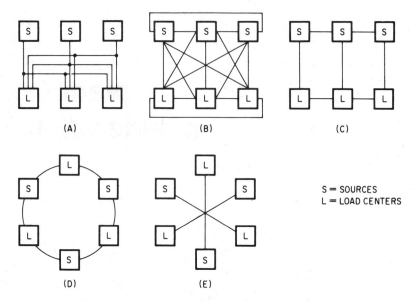

Fig. 2-1 Some basic configurations of electric transmission systems.

tion or modification of the systems shown. All of the lines shown are capable of being deenergized individually and separately. Underground portions of these lines have been operating at voltages up to 500 kV, with experimental lines operating at values up to 1,000 kV.

Distribution Layouts: Primary Supply

Distribution circuits are similar to overhead designs, except the installation is underground. Primary mains, with takeoffs, are installed, to which are connected the distribution transformers supplying low-voltage (120 to 240 V) service to consumers. Such circuit designs may vary from a simple single-feed source to the more complex involving the meshing of several feed sources.

Radial Systems

Primary circuits, having a single source of supply, are generally referred to as radial systems; circuits "radiate" from a substation source, each circuit supplying a particular area. Spurs or laterals are connected to the primary main through fuses, similar to what is done in overhead circuits, so that a fault on these laterals will not cause an interruption to the entire feeder (Fig. 2-2). Such radial circuits, very

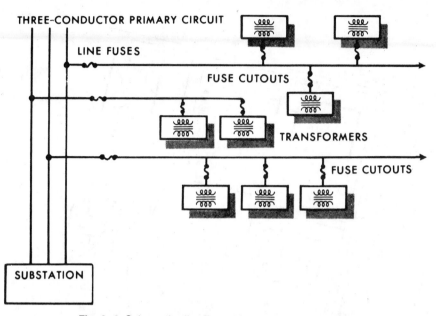

THREE-CONDUCTOR PRIMARY CIRCUIT

LINE FUSES

FUSE CUTOUTS

TRANSFORMERS

FUSE CUTOUTS

SUBSTATION

Fig. 2–2 Schematic diagram of fused three-conductor primary line supplying several distribution transformers having individual fuse cutouts.

economical both to install and operate, are widely used in overhead systems, but have limited application in underground systems.

Open-Loop Systems

In order to shorten the duration of service interruptions, the primary supply may often be arranged in the pattern of an open loop. In this instance, the section of the primary on which a fault may occur can be disconnected at both ends and service reestablished by closing the loop at the point where it is normally left open. Such loops are not normally closed because a fault on a section of the feed may cause the fuses at both ends to blow, leaving the entire area without supply, and no knowledge of where the fault has occurred (Fig. 2–3).

Closed-Loop Systems

In some special cases, where a higher degree of reliability is desired, the loop may be operated as a closed loop. In this case, protection is achieved by replacing the fuses with more expensive circuit

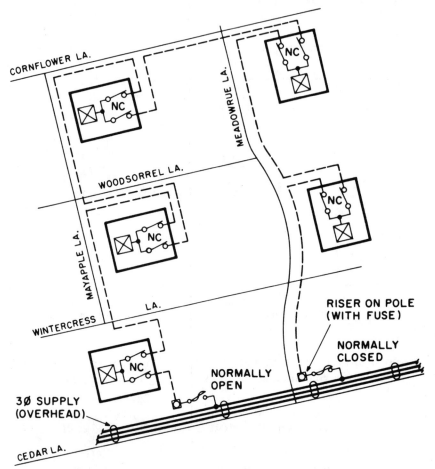

Fig. 2-3 Underground residential layout using open-loop construction.

breakers operated by relays or by a pilot wire installed from section to section of the primary feed.

Duplicate Supply Systems

In some other cases, usually involving commercial or industrial consumers, hospitals, military bases, and such, the operations carried on may be so critical as to warrant extra expenditures for firming up the supply. This may be done by having a second source installed with throw-over devices operated manually or automatically, so that, should

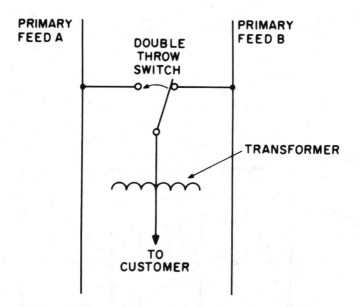

Fig. 2-4 Use of throw-over switch for extra reliability.

one source of supply fail, the service may be switched over to the alternate source (Fig. 2-4).

Secondary Network Systems

An even more complex, and expensive, method is to create a low-voltage network by connecting, through switches called protectors, the secondary mains from transformers supplied by several primary feeders. Here, should one feeder become deenergized, the power is still supplied from the others without interruption; the protectors associated with the deenergized feeder automatically open to prevent a "feedback" from the other feeders, back (through the transformers) to the de-energized feeder (Fig. 2-5).

Primary Voltages

The selection of the primary voltage to be employed depends on the loads to be supplied, length of feeders, availability of substation sites, and other local and special individual factors. Approximate voltages (line to ground) usually employed are 2,300 V (4,000 V between phases), 7,620 V (13,200 V), 13,200 V (23,000V), and 19,900 V (34,500 V); or by voltage classes: 5 kV, 15 kV, 25 kV, and 35 kV, with 15 kV presently predominant. The load-hauling capability of the feeder

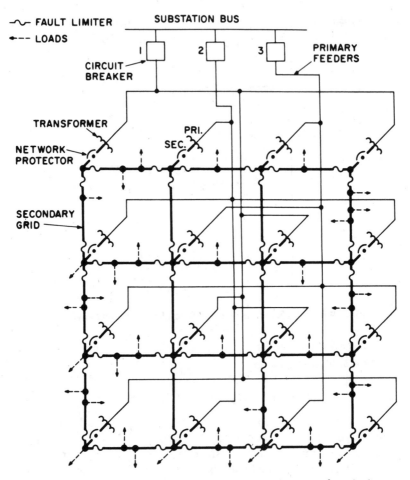

Fig. 2–5 Secondary underground network—use of protector switches to prevent feedback.

increases as the square of the ratio of voltages; e.g., the 23,000-V circuit, with a voltage 10 times that of the 2,300-V circuit, can supply 100 times the load, with the same conductor size. While the economy of the higher voltage is evident, the higher capacity of the feeder makes it possible for it to supply a greater number of consumers. In order to maintain or improve standards of service reliability, restricting the number of consumers that may be affected during a feeder interruption, it is necessary to incorporate in the feeder designs expensive switching for sectionalizing and feeder extensions to enable emergency supply from adjacent feeders.

Further, at the higher voltages, equipment connected to the lines is subject to greater mechanical stresses from larger short-circuit currents flowing under fault conditions. These include not only transformers, but protective devices including fuses and switches for sectionalizing, disconnecting lines and transformers, for opening and closing loops, etc.; these are not only more costly, but potentially less reliable. The final choice of operating voltage, therefore, is generally a compromise of many factors, including future requirements, which provide for safety, economy, and reliability.

Distribution Layouts: Transformers, Secondary Mains, and Services

One design pattern has as the primary supply a distribution transformer that may feed two or more consumers via secondary mains and services; advantage is taken of diversity between consumers' peak loads, which enables a lesser total capacity of transformers to be installed (Fig. 2–6).

Another pattern has as the primary supply an individual transformer feeding two or more consumers via service conductors only; the same diversity advantage is obtained, but perhaps to a lesser degree. Economy is achieved from the elimination of secondary mains. This pattern can be readily adapted to the single transformer per consumer, described below.

Still a third pattern has as the primary supply an individual transformer feeding only one consumer; no secondary mains are required, and the service connection to the consumer may be practically eliminated by placing the transformer adjacent to the consumers' service equipment. Further, the transformer, acting as a demand-limiting device, between the utility and the consumer, can make possible economies in the associated metering and billing operations (Fig. 2–7).

Generally, in addition to the economy of eliminating secondary mains, the single-transformer installations affect one or a few consumers, while the transformer is deenergized for any reason. On the other hand, while savings in transformer capacity, because of diversity in serving a number of consumers, may be reduced by the addition of secondary mains, a relatively large number of consumers are affected when the supply transformer becomes deenergized. The selection of the design again is based on safety, economy, service reliability, and future requirements.

In any of the configurations considered, provision is made to supply street lighting, traffic control signals, public parking illumination, direction and warning signs, and other similar requirements. This may

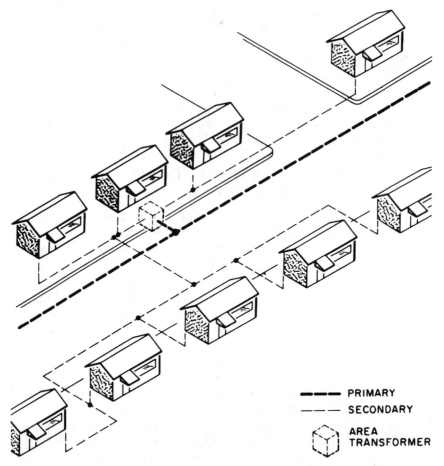

Fig. 2–6 Underground residential layout using an area transformer.

be done by supplying them from individual transformers, much like other services, or from other existing transformers by means of separate secondary mains and services.

Underground Construction

In planning underground systems, the nature of the area to be served and the methods of construction should be considered. In congested areas where digging may be difficult, cables and equipment may be installed in ducts and manholes to facilitate maintenance and replacement. In other areas the cables may be installed directly in the

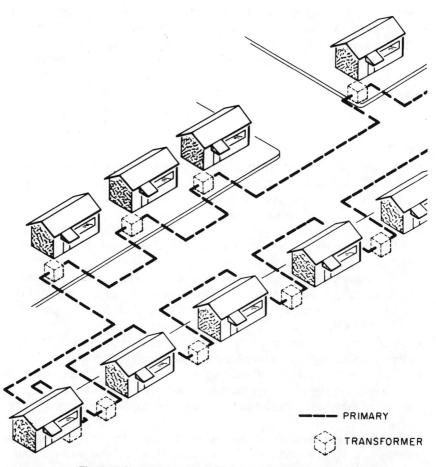

PRIMARY

TRANSFORMER

Fig. 2-7 Underground residential layout using individual transformers.

ground, saving the cost of building conduits and manholes, and allowing the use of long sections of cable, thereby eliminating the need for a number of splices. The cable may be buried alone in a trench, or may be buried together with other facilities, including telephone cables, CATV cables, gas mains, and water and sewer systems. Sharing the cost of installing such facilities can contribute greatly to the economy of underground distribution systems (see Fig. 1–4). Where only one cable is involved, it may be plowed directly in the ground, saving the cost of trenching and back-filling.

Such underground installations may be made in the street area, near the curb line, or in the area between the curb and sidewalk; they may be made along rear-lot lines common to buildings on either side. In rural areas, they may be installed in open fields or along the highway. Where such systems cross streets or highways, garage driveways, rail systems, or where other impediments exist that may subject the cables to frequent hazards, or to extraordinary construction costs, ducts may be installed and the cable threaded therein as illustrated in Fig. 1–4.

Review

- Because of the usually greater time required for restoration of underground facilities, in event of failure, it is often necessary to adopt more costly designs; the degree of complexity and cost depending on the desired standard of service reliability.
- Because of the importance of transmission systems, multiple installation of facilities is often specified, frequently from different sources and via separate alternate routes.
- Distribution circuits consist of primary mains, with take-offs, to which are connected the distribution transformers supplying low-voltage (120 to 240 V) service to consumers; primary voltage classes may be 5, 15, 25, and 35 kV.
- Primary circuits, having a single source of supply are called "radial" circuits, radiating from a substation to supply a particular area.
- To shorten the duration of interruptions, the primary supply may be arranged as an open loop; the faulted section can be disconnected at both ends and service reestablished by closing the loop where normally open (Fig. 2–3).
- Closed loops are sometimes used where a higher degree of reliability is desired; disconnection of the faulted section is done automatically through the use of more expensive breakers operated by relays or pilot wires.
- Duplicate primary supply with throw-over devices operated manually or automatically, is often employed at critical installations, so that, should one source of supply fail, service may be switched to the alternate source (Fig. 2–4).
- A more complex and expensive method creates a low-voltage network by connecting, through switches called protectors, the secondary mains from transformers supplied by several primary feeders.
- Distribution transformers may be connected to the primary supply in three ways: (1) a transformer may feed two or more consumers via secondary mains and services, taking maximum advantage of diversity between consumer peak loads, enabling a lesser total capacity of transformers to be installed (Fig. 2–6); (2) a transformer may feed two or

more consumers via services only, taking advantage of some diversity, but eliminating the secondary mains; and, (3) a transformer supplying only one consumer, with no secondary mains, and enabling it to be located adjacent to service equipment—here a failure of the transformer affects only the one consumer (Fig. 2–7).

Study Questions

1. What is a radial primary system? What are its advantages? Disadvantages?
2. What are some other primary circuit designs, and why?
3. What are some advantages of loop systems? Disadvantages?
4. What factors determine the selection of primary voltages? What are some values presently employed?
5. What is meant by "diversity"?
6. What are some transformer-secondary layouts and considerations?
7. What is a low-voltage secondary network? Where is it used?
8. What factors should be considered in planning underground systems?
9. Where may ducts and manholes be used?
10. How may street lighting, traffic signals, etc., be supplied in a URD system?

3

design
considerations

Where general appearance, economics, congestion, or maintenance conditions make overhead construction inadvisable, underground construction is specified. Overhead lines have ordinarily been considered to be less expensive and easier to maintain. While this remains particularly true of transmission lines, developments in cables, transformers, and other equipment designed for underground distribution applications together with improved methods of construction and operation have narrowed the cost gap to the point where such systems become attractive in urban and suburban residential installations, which constitute the bulk of the distribution systems.

Cables

Cables can be either single-conductor or multiple-conductor; that is, two, three, or four conductors may be enclosed in a single protective sheath. Putting two or more conductors into one sheath is an economic measure, since only one cable is handled, rather than several, when they are installed in a trench or duct, and only one sheath is necessary. Where the cable may be tapped rather frequently, as in service connections, secondary or primary distribution mains, and street-lighting facilities, single-conductor cables are generally used because of the ease in making the necessary splices. Multiple-conductor cables are usually used for main-line portions of transmission lines and distribution circuits where few or no taps or takeoffs exist (Fig. 3–1).

The conductors are generally made of copper or aluminum, and are stranded or compacted, except for the smaller sizes, to make the

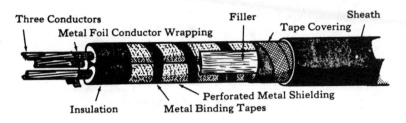

Fig. 3-1 An underground cable.

cable more flexible and easier to handle. The size is specified in circular mils or in American Wire Gage numbers, exactly the same as for overhead conductors.

Where the copper conductor is to make contact with rubber insulation, the conductor or its strands are coated with tin to prevent chemical action between the metal and the sulfur contained in the rubber insulation.

Plastic insulation is applied to the conductor under pressure, the thickness of the material around the conductor depending on the voltage rating of the cable, usually somewhat higher than that at which the cable will operate. Such insulations on primary cables, at present, may consist of cross-linked polyethylene, ethylene propylene rubber, or polyethylene, and have been successfully used in cables rated for application up to 138 kV; research and development will no doubt raise this level in future cables. For higher-voltage applications, paper insulation is wrapped around the conductor and impregnated with oil before the sheath is applied. Butyl rubber is sometimes used for secondary cables, operating at 600 V or less.

Especially when buried directly in the ground, cables must be sheathed for protection from mechanical injury during installation, from moisture, gases, chemicals, and other damaging substances in the soil or atmosphere. Earlier sheaths were almost always made of lead because of its moisture-proof and good mechanical buffering qualities, but these sheaths were subject to corrosion and insect and rodent damage and were costly. New types of plastic that do not deteriorate from exposure to any weather, sunlight, moisture, and chemicals have largely taken the place of the more expensive and less flexible lead sheathing. Earlier neoprene, polyethylene, and polyvinylchloride (PVC) sheaths have given way to plastics compounded to meet the more demanding particular needs of direct-burial installations (Fig. 3-2).

All cables are subject to thermal expansion from the loading and unloading of current during daily or other period cycles, which initiate

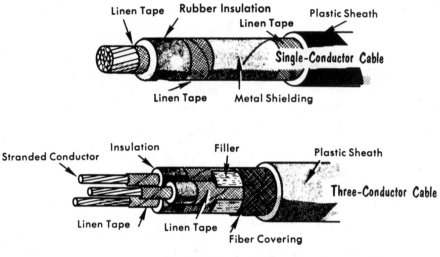

Fig. 3–2 Types of cable.

motion with respect to the insulation. Such motion, due to loading variations, tends to cause the formation of voids or pockets in the insulation. A void between the conductor and the insulation, or between the insulation and the grounded shielding tape or metallic sheath, may also be formed due to faulty manufacturing, bending too sharply during installation, or from other causes. Such minute air pockets, under the electrostatic forces of the energized conductor, tend to ionize, that is, become conductors of electricity (see Fig. 3–3A). This ionization of minute particles within the void causes corona discharge, which results in minute scorching and carbonization of the adjacent insulation. This is the beginning of "tracking" and the creation of ozone, which damages the insulating value of most compounds (see Fig. 3–3B). When sufficient numbers of these air pockets form, a tracking or charred path occurs where the insulation breaks down. Ultimately, the insulation is bridged with a carbonized track that is conductive and the cable fails (see Fig. 3–3C).

Transmission Cables

Transmission cables present particular problems. The high voltages at which these cables operate cause a high degree of ionization of the voids, which becomes especially destructive. The "skin effect" of alternating current tends to make the greater part of the current flowing in a conductor flow in the outer part of the conductor nearer the surface,

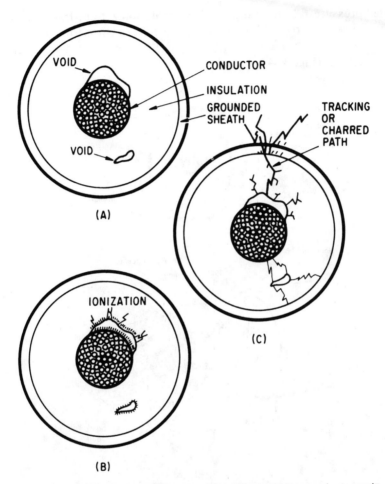

Fig. 3-3 Tracking in a cable. (A) Void between the conductor and the insulation. (B) Corona discharge. (C) Cable failure.

causing additional heat to be generated in those parts, and further aggravating the destructive effect mentioned earlier.

Pressure-Type Cables

To counteract some of this destructive effect, cables are designed with a hollow core into which oil or gas (usually nitrogen, but sometimes SF_6, sulfur hexafluoride) under pressure is introduced. The theory here is that, when voids in the insulation do occur, the oil or gas under pressure fills the voids and prevents ionization, tracking, and failure. These hollow cables are sometimes referred to as Emanueli type, after their inventor, but more often as Pirelli cables after their principal manufacturer (Fig. 3–4).

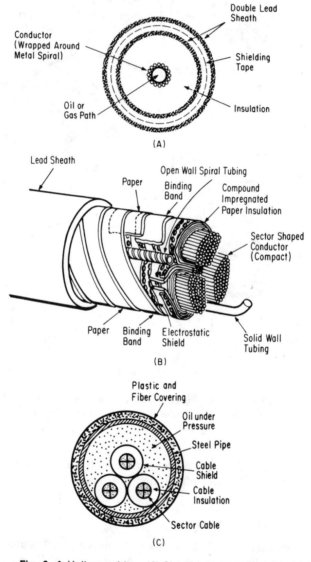

Fig. 3–4 Hollow cables. (A) Single conductor or Pirelli type. (B) Three-conductor oil or gas filled. (C) Pipe type (pressure).

Another application of the same principle employs "solid-type" cables installed in a pipe in which the oil or gas under pressure surrounds the conductors and insulation. To differentiate between this type and the hollow core cables, these are sometimes referred to as "oil-static" (for oil-filled), or, more generally, "pipe-type" cables.

These cables have been used in circuits operating from 69 kV to upwards of 500 kV. Special accessories and auxiliary equipment to handle the oil or gas are needed with these type cables.

Stop-Joints

In long installations, it is obvious that an oil or gas leak in either the hollow or pipe cable systems could lead to a long and costly decontamination process. To restrict the possibility of widespread contamination, such systems are usually sectionalized through the insertion of stop-joints and semistop-joints in the cable system. The number and types of such joints is usually dependent on the length of the line and its importance. The stop-joint provides a physical barrier to both the conductor and the oil or gas flow system (Fig. 3–5). These are used on long transmission lines and permit the line to be sectionalized so that the cables may be repaired or replaced without affecting the entire length of line. The semistop-joint allows the conductor to pass through but imposes a physical barrier to the oil or gas flow system. Hence, in the event of a leak that would allow air or another contaminant to enter the cable, only a relatively small section of the line between the semistop-joints is affected. In repairing such cables, only the oil or gas in one of the sections is completely replaced, holding down both the time for repair and decontamination and the cost for such an incident.

Such cable installations require extraordinary care, since the surfaces that come into contact with the insulating oil or gas must be free from contamination. Evacuation, of the hollow-cored conductor or the pipe containing the solid-type cables, before the introduction of the oil or gas, therefore, requires a high degree of vacuum and cleanliness. Double sheaths, sandwiching a metallic shielding tape, on hollow-type cables and special coverings on the pipe for pipe-type cables are used to mitigate or prevent corrosion, electrolysis, and other damage. Obviously, such installations, while varying with the type of construction, nature of the terrain, road surface, transportation, and other factors, are extremely expensive. Costs may range from 5 to as high as 20 to 30 times (averaging 8 to 10 times) the cost of overhead installations.

For lower voltages, solid-type insulated cables are used, and the information applying to distribution cables also apply to these ratings of transmission cables.

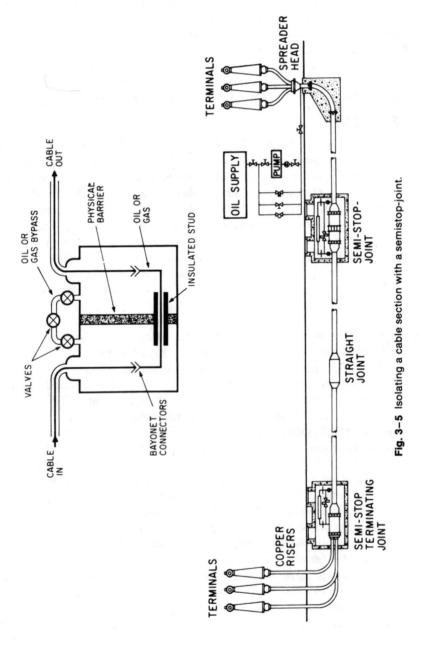

Fig. 3–5 Isolating a cable section with a semistop-joint.

Charging Currents

In underground transmission systems, the high voltage and the configuration of the conductor and sheath or pipe produce a condenser action. This is intensified as voltage levels increase, resulting in so-called charging currents that may exceed the cable thermal limits. This occurs if the length of the cable is sufficiently great, which makes the amount of current necessary to "charge" the cable rather large, thereby reducing its load-carrying capability. In instances where voltage levels are on the order of 345 kV or greater, total depletion of the load-carrying ability may occur after some 30 miles of transmission. Corrective equipment is available to compensate for this energy loss, but at extremely high cost. This cost must be added to the high cost of underground cable, the cost of splicing, which requires special skills, and other costs associated with underground installations. Much technical progress is still necessary to make such underground high-voltage transmission installations competitive with overhead transmission installations.

Distribution Cables

Cables for distribution systems are relatively simple in design, consisting usually of a nonhollow conductor, solid or stranded, surrounded by insulation, usually oil-impregnated paper, varnished cambric, rubber, or suitable plastic compounds. Sheaths of lead, almost universal, are giving way to suitable plastics.

Primary Cables

Where the primary supply consists of an energized conductor and a neutral, the installation may consist of an insulated cable and a bare conductor, but very often, these two are combined into one, with the neutral wrapped concentrically over a semiconducting layer around the insulated cable (Fig. 3–6). Mechanically, this one cable is easier to

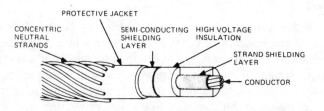

Fig. 3–6 Primary concentric neutral underground cable.

handle than two, and the neutral acts as protection for the cable against abrasion during installation; electrically, the concentric cable results in less voltage drop because of reduced reactance, and the neutral acts as an electrostatic shield around the cable tending to make more uniform the electrostatic voltage stresses within the insulation. The neutral conductor may consist of circular shaped strands, or flat-strap or ribbon-shaped strands. Because it is exposed to corrosion and electrolytic action from chemicals and stray currents in the soil, the entire cable is sometimes covered by an insulating jacket, not only protecting the metallic strands, but preventing interference to nearby communication circuits from the corroded neutrals.

Secondary Cables

Similarly, secondary conductors may consist of one or more insulated cables and a neutral conductor, or each cable may have a neutral wrapped concentrically around it; often two conductors are placed together into an oval-shaped cable, and the neutral wrapped concentrically around the two-conductor cable. The concentric neutral may be exposed, or may be jacketed, similar to the primary cable (Fig. 3–7).

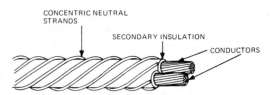

Fig. 3–7 Secondary concentric twin underground cable.

As an additional means of field identification for cables, the flat-strap or ribbon neutrals are specified for primary cables (Fig. 3–8), and circular strands for secondary cables (see Fig. 3–4).

Splices

Either primary or secondary cables may be spliced by joining the conductors mechanically, usually by a sleeve into which the ends of the two conductors are placed and crimped by means of a compressing tool. Tape, similar to the plastic insulation, is wound around the connection to the proper specified thickness. Semiconducting or metallic foil tape is wound about the insulation and a final protection tape or sheath, similar to the plastic sheath, is wound over the entire splice. The concentric neutrals are spread apart from the cable, bundled together into an approximate circular shape and spliced together mechanically as are the other conductors; they may also be covered by a plastic tape to protect them from corrosion and electrolytic action (Fig. 3–9).

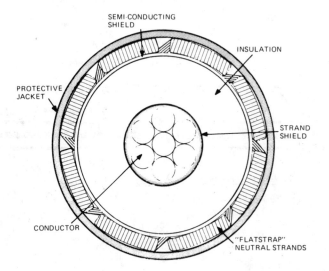

Fig. 3–8 Typical flat strap-type primary cable construction.

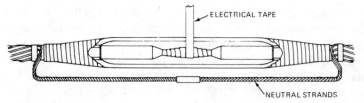
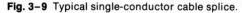

Fig. 3–9 Typical single-conductor cable splice.

When three-conductor (three-phase) cables are spliced together, care should be taken that the particular phase conductors in one cable are connected to the corresponding phase conductors in the other cable. Cables may also be connected using premolded plastic splices. The conductors are connected in the same manner as described above. However, the two halves of a premolded plastic sleeve or sheath are each slipped over the ends of the cables before the conductors are spliced, then brought together and sealed at each end by plastic tape; the space inside is then filled, through a hole in the sleeves, with melted plastic insulation under pressure (one hole acting as an air hole allowing the plastic to drive out the air which it replaces), and allowed to cool. The neutrals are handled in the same manner (Fig. 3–10).

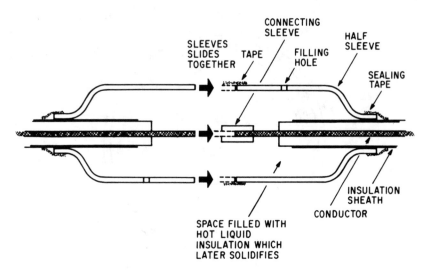

Fig. 3–10 Premolded plastic splice, single-conductor, compression type.

Where more than two cables are spliced together, similar techniques are employed, with some modification. A preinsulated wye connection, to which three conductors are connected, has three "half" sleeves which are taped to a premolded covering, and filled with melted plastic, as in the joints described above. Similar joints are used for four conductors (Fig. 3–11).

In some cases, the cables are not spliced together directly, but are connected to a terminal containing a number of stud connectors and the terminal and studs covered by molded insulation. The insulation and sheath of the cables are taped to the insulation and molded covering of the studs. In other cases, the terminal may contain a number of molded-insulated load-break elbows and bushings. Here the cable is connected to a plastic- or porcelain-covered stud, which fits into a plastic- or porcelain-covered receptacle to make the connection; the stud may be pulled, by means of an insulated hook stick, from the receptacle, which may be energized (Fig. 3–12). These may be used to connect or disconnect one primary feed to another whether energized or deenergized; for

Fig. 3-11 Premolded typical "T" splice assembly or "wye" joint.

Fig. 3-12 Typical load break elbow terminator and bushing connection.

example, in opening or closing a loop circuit or connecting or disconnecting a transformer.

In some cases, the molded terminal may be combined with the terminals of a transformer or switch. As mentioned in the preceding chapter, these may serve as test points on an open-loop circuit in restoring service after an interruption; the faulted section being disconnected at both ends by pulling the studs from the receptacles, and the two remaining unfaulted parts of the loop reenergized at both ends.

Transformers

Transformers for such underground systems may be installed above the ground on concrete or plastic pads (Fig. 3–13), partially above and partially below ground in low-profile semiburied vaults or receptacles, in completely buried vaults or receptacles, in manholes, or buried directly in the ground. Where transformers are installed or buried completely below ground, markers of metal, plastic, or concrete may be installed on the ground or on short stubs above the ground to indicate their location.

The transformers may be designed for underground operation, or may be overhead transformers modified to be installed semiunderground on pads, or underground in vaults or receptacles, but not buried directly in the ground; the overhead transformers are used in temporary or other situations in which such installations may be expedient, but such installations are not recommended.

Underground transformers are hermetically sealed against moisture, and this includes the terminals and bushings. As mentioned earlier, the terminals can contain two or more insulated disconnecting elbows, enabling a simple and flexible means for sectionalizing circuits or disconnecting transformers during fault conditions. Generally, the transformers are installed in an upright position, with the terminals on the top or sides of the unit; one type, designed for direct burial in the trench made by the cable-burying equipment, is installed on its side, rather than in the upright position.

Those installed on ground-level pads, or in semiburied pads, sometimes have their connections made behind a protective panel, with only the insulated disconnecting handles protruding, so that when the enclosure is opened, no energized part is exposed; these are known as "dead-front" transformers, in contrast to those in which energized parts may be exposed when the enclosure is opened (Fig. 3–14).

The transformers may be of the completely self-protected (CSP) type with an internal primary weak link and secondary breakers, or of the conventional type, in which case they are usually associated with oil-fuse cutouts, oil, or vacuum switches. Where necessary, lightning arresters may be installed but in most cases are not necessary in underground systems. The transformers may also have primary taps, similar to overhead units.

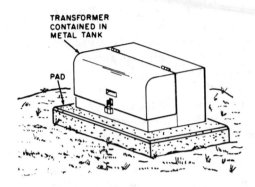

Fig. 3–13 Pad-mounted transformer.

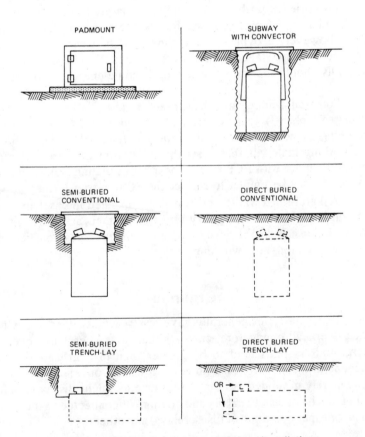

Fig. 3–14 Typical underground transformer installations.

Transformer Tanks

Transformer tanks may be made of steel, and may be painted or provided with a plastic coating to prevent or retard corrosion from chemical action or electrolytic action due to stray currents. Where such precautions are insufficient, sacrificial anodes may be connected to the case and buried in the ground; the anode, while consuming itself, creates an electrolytic action that causes currents to flow to the tank, rather than away from it, preventing the flow of metal ions away from the tank, which usually causes corrosion.

The transformer tanks are usually connected to the neutral conductors, and often with a separate connection to another ground, for safety purposes should the tank somehow become energized and the connection to the neutral become open or defective. In areas where corrosion problems are serious, the tanks of transformers, which are located completely below ground level, either completely enclosed or completely buried in earth, or are installed below ground partially buried in earth and the upper part enclosed, may not be connected to the system neutral; however, a bypass shunt connected between the tank and system neutral is installed, which causes the tank to be grounded automatically should the transformer tank become energized for any reason.

Some oils and askarels have been found to contain PCB (polycholrinated biphenyl), a cancer causing substance. It may be eliminated by draining the contaminated fluids, flushing the transformer with special absorbing materials that draw the PCB from the core and other parts, and replace with PCB-free oil or other insulating fluids. In some instances, it may be simpler to replace the existing transformer.

Askarel-filled transformers may be installed in cases in which fire hazards are to be avoided. Dry-type transformers are also used, but their insulation is less capable of sustaining voltage surges from lightning (near riser locations) or switching.

Grounds

Because cables generally have less reactance than the wider-spaced overhead conductors, currents that flow when faults occur in underground systems tend to be greater than in overhead systems. Hence, neutral conductors should not only be of proper size, but should be adequately grounded, so that fault currents might dissipate before causing much damage to cables and equipment connected to them, and to insure proper operation of fuses, relays, and other protective devices.

Where possible, the neutral conductors should be connected to other metallic underground structures and to driven grounds. In this regard, it should be noted that water pipe grounds should be supplemented by driven grounds, since the use of nonconducting pipe in water supply systems no longer provides a good trustworthy ground source.

Protective Devices

Fuses are placed so that they may disconnect a portion of a circuit that may be faulted, allowing the rest of the circuit to remain energized. They may also be connected between the primary line and the transformer to protect the transformer from overloads, and to disconnect the transformer from the primary in case of trouble. For underground service, the fuses are generally contained in watertight receptacles filled with oil, usually referred to as oil-filled cutouts. Fuses in vacuum are also employed. Both types tend to quench any arcs that may develop by depriving them of air (oxygen), which tends to sustain them. Because of the heavy fault currents they may be called upon to handle, even for very short periods of time, they are of rugged construction; both of these features make them considerably more expensive than their overhead counterparts.

Switches may be used to disconnect portions of a circuit from other segments of the same circuit or to other circuits to reestablish service in times of fault. For the same reasons as mentioned above, the contacts of the switches are contained in watertight receptacles filled with oil. More recently, the contacts may be contained in a vacuum. Both the oil-filled and vacuum switches operate similarly to the same type fuses when the contacts are open under load, the arcs being deprived of air (oxygen) which sustains them. Both are designed to operate while energized or deenergized; they may be remotely controlled as well as manually operated.

Reclosers, which are essentially oil switches actuated by relays, are set to reclose the switch a predetermined number of times after predetermined intervals of time, before locking themselves open for manual operation. These are usually installed where a portion of the circuit is overhead, and serve to protect against temporary faults (usually on the overhead portion) locking out the circuit.

Lightning arresters protect cables, transformers, and other equipment from voltage surges resulting from lightning or improper switching of a circuit. They are generally not required for underground installations, except at risers where such underground cables may connect to overhead facilities. In some special instances, they may also be installed at transformer or equipment installations, usually close to the riser location, which may be affected by the voltage surges. They are usually installed with the transformer, or other equipment they are to protect, in the same enclosure or vault (Fig. 3–15).

All of these devices may be installed on ground level or below ground pads, sometimes with transformers or other equipment, suitably provided with protective covers (see Fig. 3–11). They may also be installed in vaults or receptacles below ground. Occasionally, overhead-type devices may be installed in above-ground enclosures, as a matter of economy, where safety and proper operation of the devices are assured.

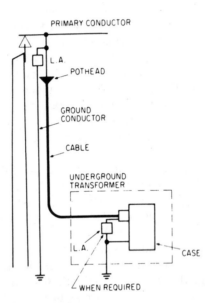

PRIMARY CONDUCTOR

L.A.

POTHEAD

GROUND CONDUCTOR

CABLE

UNDERGROUND TRANSFORMER

L.A.

CASE

WHEN REQUIRED

Fig. 3–15 Lightning arrester on riser connected to underground transformer.

Ducts and Manholes

There are many occasions when it may not be desirable to bury cables in the ground, in urban and built-up areas where streets are paved, for example. In such cases, resort is had to the use of ducts (or conduits) and manholes, a more costly and complex procedure.

In planning a duct system, in addition to economics, other practical considerations should be taken into account. Length of duct runs, bends, depth and kind of terrain in which they are to be installed, the size and number of manholes involved, not only to supply the customers, but to accommodate the feeders and mains required, to obtain proper separation of facilities for reliability, the interferences that may be encountered, present and future requirements, all contribute to the final selection of design.

Ducts

The number and size of ducts to be installed are determined by the present requirement for such facilities, together with the probable need for a reasonable future time (usually 10 years, but determined by economics) and the maximum number of ducts that are desirable and allowable in a single duct bank. In some cases, it may be desirable to add one or more "extra" ducts to complete a layer of the regular duct formation.

The maximum (or optimum) limit for the number of ducts to be built in a given section is determined by balancing the desire to secure additional duct space at a low cost against the unreliability of placing too many cables in one duct bank (and manhole), which can result in their becoming overheated.

When cables are crowded together in a multiple-duct bank, the heat radiation from a particular cable may be so reduced that the overall total current-carrying capacity of all the cables in the duct bank is actually less than the total current-carrying capacity of the same size cables less in number in a smaller bank. The cables occupying those lower-cost ducts must be operated with lower heat losses, thereby tending to offset the low-cost incremental construction and reduce the effectiveness of the overall cable and duct investment. The presence of other subsurface structures may restrict the location of new or additional duct banks, and may result in the crowding of new duct banks in that area, thereby reducing the cooling capacity of the surrounding earth.

Also, where too many ducts enter a manhole at one point, the congestion of cables becomes intolerable; it may be more desirable to build one or more additional separate duct lines with their own separate manholes. In general, the load-carrying ability of cables (the safe maximum operating temperature) will depend on their position in the duct bank; it will decrease in the inner ducts and increase in the outer ones.

The relative advantages and disadvantages of several typical duct bank arrangements are indicated in Table 3–1. In some cases, a given design may be found satisfactory for one type of transmission and distribution supply, but completely unsatisfactory for another; if the

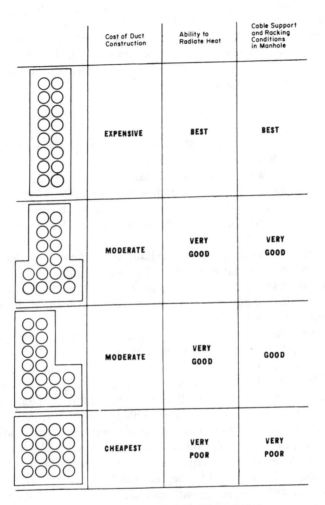

	Cost of Duct Construction	Ability to Radiate Heat	Cable Support and Racking Conditions in Manhole
	EXPENSIVE	BEST	BEST
	MODERATE	VERY GOOD	VERY GOOD
	MODERATE	VERY GOOD	GOOD
	CHEAPEST	VERY POOR	VERY POOR

Table 3-1. Comparative Duct Characteristics.

normal capacity of some cables is limited, it may place restrictions on other parts of the circuit, including such items as cables, transformers, switches, etc., not permitting the full realization of their capacity and investment. In many cases, however, the available horizontal and vertical space, considering the existence of other underground utilities, may dictate the final arrangement and dimensions of the duct bank installed.

The most commonly used ducts are made of precast concrete, transite (a fireproof-based compound), tile, fiber, plastic, and steel pipe (Fig. 3-16). Ducts installed under roadways or other places subject to

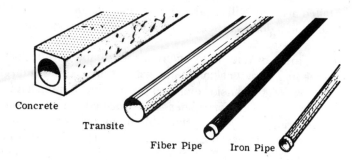

Concrete

Transite

Fiber Pipe   Iron Pipe

Fig. 3-16 Underground cable is carried and protected by different types of ducts or conduits.

severe loading are usually made of steel and may be encased in concrete. Ducts are usually installed in the ground below the frost line, but at a minimum ordinarily of 2 to 3 feet to provide for safe dispersion of concentrated pressures that may be applied at the street surface. Ducts may be spaced 2 to 3 inches apart, whether in earth or concrete. While the grade of the duct line depends largely on the natural or established grade of the street surface, duct lines should be designed so that they drain toward the manholes (Fig. 3-17).

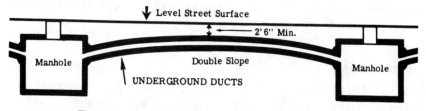

↓ Level Street Surface

2'6" Min.

Manhole   Double Slope   Manhole

↑ UNDERGROUND DUCTS

Fig. 3-17 One way of grading a conduit between manholes.

Good practice ordinarily requires that sufficient clearance be provided between the cable, or cables, to be installed and the walls of the duct. The minimum clearance will depend on the length of the duct run, the size (diameter) of the duct, the number and curvature of bends, and the quality and alignment of the duct sections. In general, the duct diameter should be at least ½ inch larger than the cable, or the (imaginary) circle enclosing several cables, where such may be installed. In special cases, however, as in a single cable installed in a straight, clear duct, a lesser clearance may be acceptable provided the pulling stresses do not approach values that will result in damage to the cable. A single cable installed in a duct will require less tension, weight for weight, than several cables in a duct, particularly when they are heavy and of large size.

Curvatures of duct lines should permit cables to be installed without exceeding a practical minimum installation bending radius limit of some 8 to 10 times the outside diameter of the cable (although this may be reduced to about half for rubber- or varnished cambric-insulated cables). In general, the degree of curvature in duct lines should be kept as low as possible. It has been found, however, that with radii of curvature greater than about 300 feet and with ample clearances between cable and duct, the effect of the curvature on cable-pulling tension is not very great and may be neglected. With decreasing clearances, curvatures in the duct assume greater importance; the length of the curvature and its radius affect the cable-pulling tension. Reverse curves on long duct runs should be avoided wherever possible.

Ducts may also be installed in conjunction with direct-burial cable systems. Where cables may be buried in the ground, prior to known future paving, "spare" plastic duct or ducts may be installed alongside the cables, to provide for future installation of a new cable (and abandoning of the old) in event of fault. In other instances, such as crossings, corners, driveways, etc., ducts made of steel pipe or of flexible steel corrugated tubing are sometimes installed.

In some special instances, cables may be placed in precast concrete troughs located under sidewalks, with the sidewalk slabs acting as covers for the troughs.

Manholes

The design of manholes for long cable runs is based primarily on the necessity of providing for the relatively large amount of expansion and contraction that results from the variation in the load currents carried by the conductors. While this provision can be taken care of in several different ways, one popular and effective method is to provide a large reverse curve in the cable passing through the manhole. This reverse curve, consisting of two large radius 90° bends, enables the cable to take up the expansion movements and reduces to a minimum the danger of cracking or buckling the sheath. This arrangement may be accomplished by bringing the ducts into the manhole at opposite corners.

The proper selection of manhole locations should not only reduce to a minimum the necessity of curved duct alignment, but should take into account changes in street grades, to permit ducts to drain toward the manholes, as mentioned earlier.

Where only a few ducts are required (for primary feeders or secondary mains to serve only the local distribution system, for example), smaller manholes (sometimes referred to as pull or distribution boxes) may be specified, particularly when the cables installed are small in diameter and easily supported or racked. In such manholes, head room is either reduced to a height sufficient for the workers to operate without excessive cramping, or completely eliminated with the resulting shallow box permitting the workman to operate from the ground.

The size of the manhole opening, or shaft through the manhole roof, varies with the size and type of manhole. The opening should be large enough to allow workers to enter, even when a ladder may have to be placed at an extreme angle. Also, the opening, or openings, should be large enough to permit all equipment, including transformers, for underground service to pass through readily. For shallower boxes, the openings should permit workers to operate safely, with sufficient space to enable them to perform without undue hindrance from crowding of facilities or other encumbrances.

The type, shape, and size of a manhole depend on many conditions: location, whether at an intersection or between road corners; size

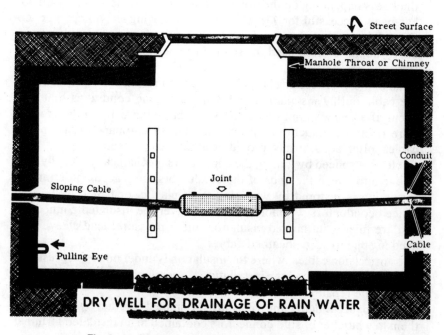

Fig. 3–18 Typical manhole with dry well.

and type of cables to be carried through the manhole; location of gas or water pipes, or other subsurface structures; and it should be large and deep enough to provide working space and head room and drainage for duct lines. The dimensions of a manhole (including the size of the manhole opening) are also determined by the number of ducts and the different levels on which they enter the manhole, the type of cable to be racked, the length of the splice, and by other equipment (switches, transformers, etc.) that may be installed. Manholes are generally built of reinforced concrete and may be precast or poured in place; covers are usually made of steel. Drainage to sewers or dry wells may also be provided (Fig. 3–18).

Review

- Cables can be either single-conductor or multiple-conductor, that is, two, three, or four conductors enclosed within a single sheath for economy. Conductors may be of copper or aluminum, and stranded or compacted; their size is specified in circular mils or American Wire Gage number (Fig. 3–2).
- Insulation generally consists of plastic applied to the conductor, the thickness depending on the voltage rating of the cable. Such insulation has been successful for 138-kV operation; for higher voltage application, oil-impregnated paper under continuous oil or gas pressure is used; butyl rubber is often used for secondary cables operating at 600 V or less.
- Lead or plastic sheathing is applied over the insulation for protection of the cable during installation and from damaging conditions that may occur after installation, especially when buried directly in the ground. Bare neutral conductors, wrapped around the primary or secondary cables, often act as armor providing additional protection.
- Cables are spliced by joining the conductors mechanically, usually by a sleeve into which the ends of the conductors are placed and crimped. Insulation is restored by wrapping tape, plastic, or paper around the spliced conductors. Premolded sleeves cover the insulated connection and are filled with melted insulation under pressure; lead sleeves are used in splicing lead-sheathed cables.
- In transmission cables, where the insulation is under oil or gas pressure, stop-joints are used in long installations to sectionalize the cable system to facilitate repair (Fig. 3–5).
- Primary or secondary cables may also be spliced together by connecting them to a number of stud connectors contained in an insulated terminal

board. Some of these may consist of an insulated stud that fits into an insulated receptacle to make the connection, but capable of being pulled apart for disconnecting while energized; these are referred to as load-break terminals.

- Transformers may be installed above the ground on concrete or plastic pads partially above and partially below ground in low-profile semiburied vaults or receptacles, in completely buried vaults or receptacles, in manholes, or buried directly in the ground (Fig. 3–14).

- Ducts are usually made of transite or concrete, but wood, plastic, and fiber may also be used; where extra strength or rigidity are required, iron or steel pipe is used. They are usually installed deep enough to be below the frost line and to allow safe dispersion of concentrated pressures at the street surface. Curvature in duct lines should be kept as low as possible to facilitate pulling in of cables (Fig. 3–17).

- Manhole shapes and sizes depend on many conditions: location, cables to be installed, and subsurface structures. They should provide sufficient space for the workers and for the proper arrangement of cables, as well as for any equipment that may be installed; drainage for water should also be provided. Manholes are generally constructed of bricks or reinforced concrete, which may be precast into standard patterns for ease in installation.

Study Questions

1. What are the advantages of single-conductor cables? Where are they used?
2. What are the advantages of multiconductor cables? Where are they used?
3. Of what materials are cable conductors made? Why are they stranded? How are conductor sizes specified?
4. What are some of the plastic materials used for insulation in underground cables? What has been the highest voltage rating of cable to which they have been successfully applied?
5. What are some of the plastics materials used for sheathing of underground cables?
6. What is a concentric cable? What are some of its advantages?
7. How may cables be spliced?
8. What precautions should be taken in splicing three-conductor cables?
9. What are load-break elbows or bushings? Where are they used?
10. To what hazards may transformer and other equipment tanks buried in the ground be exposed?

installation considerations

The practices employed in underground construction depend largely on the type of installation to be made and the nature of the terrain. Where a multiplicity of cables and other facilities are to be installed, it may be necessary for a deep and wide trench to be excavated; in more densely populated areas, duct banks containing six or more conduits may be installed together with associated manholes. In other areas, where relatively few cables and other facilities are to be installed, a narrower trench may be sufficient. In the instances where only one or two electric underground cables are to be installed, they may be laid in a still more narrow trench or plowed into the ground.

Trenching and Plowing

The nature of the terrain plays an important part in the selection of construction methods. In rocky and stony ground, for example, it may be impractical to plow or even to cut a narrow trench, and jackhammers, concrete cutters, and hand digging may have to be utilized. On the other hand, in sandy or swampy areas, plowing may not only be practical for a few cables, but may necessitate much hand digging for larger installations and extensive shoring of the trench to keep the slides from collapsing and well points to keep the trench from filling with water where pumps are inadequate.

In digging trenches, backhoes or trenching machines, where wider trenches are called for, may be employed (Fig. 4–1). Narrow-

Fig. 4-1 Backhoe-type trenching machine.

Fig. 4-2 Narrow-cutting trenching machine.

Fig. 4–3 Vibratory cable plow.

Fig. 4–4 Typical back-fill operation.

cutting machines, sometimes known as earth saws (Fig. 4–2), may be used for digging trenches only a few inches wide; these also may sometimes be used to cut into frozen ground. Pavement or concrete breakers or jackhammers may be used where the surface is paved, or where frost has hardened the ground at the surface.

Plows may be used for digging furrows where the cables will be placed; these are used where the consistency of the ground makes them practical to achieve the specified depths, usually a minimum of about 24 inches. In cases in which the soil prevents such plows from digging the furrows to the proper depth, vibrating plows are used to facilitate the effort (Fig. 4–3). Back-fill plows, propelled by tractors or attached to other trenching machines, may be used to replace the soil into the trench or furrow (Fig. 4–4). Single or double augers may be used to dig holes that can be expanded to accommodate vaults, receptacles, transfor-

Fig. 4–5 Auger-type digger.

mers, or other equipment (Fig. 4–5). Combinations of some or all of these methods and equipment may be used, depending on the particular circumstances.

Duct and Manhole Installation

After trenches are excavated to the proper depth and graded, ducts may be installed. The bottom of the trench is leveled, smoothed, and cleared of sharp stones and other debris. If a concrete base is specified, it is poured, spaded, and leveled.

Transmission Systems

For high-voltage oil or gas-filled pressure-type transmission lines, plastic - and fiber-covered steel pipes, usually from 6 to 10 inches in diameter, are placed on precast concrete or wooden saddles and laid on the bottom of the trench. Steel pipes are welded together and joints tested for tightness. The covering is restored carefully to prevent corrosion or electrolysis from damaging the steel pipe.

Since the soil in which these pipes are buried has an important effect on the rated current-carrying capacity of the cables within, the soil must provide adequate heat dissipation to prevent overheating and failure of the cables. Slag, ashes, or porous material are poor thermal-conducting soils. Hot spots may occur, in which case the soil around that particular area may be replaced with earth or "thermal" sands having better heat-dissipating characteristics (Fig. 4–6).

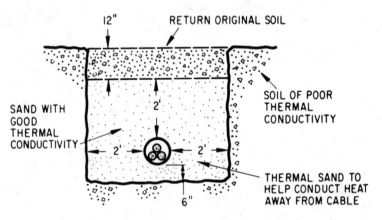

Fig. 4–6 A cable buried in underground soil.

Distribution Systems

For solid-type insulation cable installations (including lower-voltage transmission lines), ducts made of precast concrete, transite, tile, fiber, plastic, or steel are installed singly or in banks; popular duct sizes are 3, 3½, 4, and 5 inches in diameter, and sections making up the duct run may be from 5 to 10 feet in length, depending on the type and material of the duct.

Duct sections are laid in a tier to the proper number, and, where necessary, wooden or precast concrete spacers are placed to hold the duct sections at the specified separation. Duct ends are tapered, painted, or prepared with compound, as necessary, and the individual duct sections are fitted together and aligned. Joints or couplings may be of the sleeve type, or of the male–female socket type, or the sections may be butted together with a heavy glued tape wrapped around the connection, depending on the kind and type of duct being installed.

Large-radius curves may be formed from the individual straight duct sections. Short pieces are connected together with joints or couplings to form relatively smooth curves of tight and rigid construction. This is usually limited to curves where the angle between adjacent duct sections is less than about 10°. Otherwise, preformed, precast, or prefabricated bends and elbows are connected to each other or to straight sections as described above.

After the bottom layer or tier of ducts is placed, earth fill or concrete is placed on top, and the process of placing individual duct sections is repeated. Light tamping or spading is advisable to insure even distribution of earth or concrete between the ducts. The duct bank is thus built up and filled in tier by tier until the full duct structure has been completed. Care should be taken that the ducts are laid so that the section joints are staggered and do not fall in line vertically, and preferably also not in line horizontally.

After the last tier has been placed, and the concrete envelope, where specified, is completed, the earth is back-filled to the ground level. Tamping during this operation eliminates voids and pockets to prevent uneven and undue stresses on the ducts installed.

Manholes

Manholes are usually required for the purpose of pulling cable into and out of ducts, and for splicing cables, both for original installation and for repair or replacement. In this latter use, they may be installed in underground systems where cables are buried directly in the ground.

Manholes are generally constructed of reinforced concrete or brick, and the covers are made of steel. The section leading from the street to the manhole proper is usually called the "chimney" or "throat": it may also be made of reinforced concrete or brick, irrespective of the type of construction of the manhole.

Manholes of specific sizes and shapes may be cast in place at the location where they are to be installed. They are often precast into standardized patterns, or into the special sizes and shapes desired. The precast method is often the quickest, most economical way to install them, eliminating the inconveniences that often accompany the field pouring of concrete, especially in crowded areas.

Since water can accumulate at the bottom of manholes, some form of drainage should be provided. Where sewer connections can be made conveniently, this is usually done. In cases in which the bottom of the manhole is below the natural water table or in which the earth will not support the manhole structure on the wall footings alone, it is good practice to provide a concrete floor and a sump (or well) where the water can collect and drain off into a storm sewer or some other part of the ground. In many cases, the bottom of the manhole is excavated and filled with stones to make a dry well (Fig. 4–7).

There are areas where the soil is so moist and the water table so high that manholes should be made as waterproof as possible. Along the

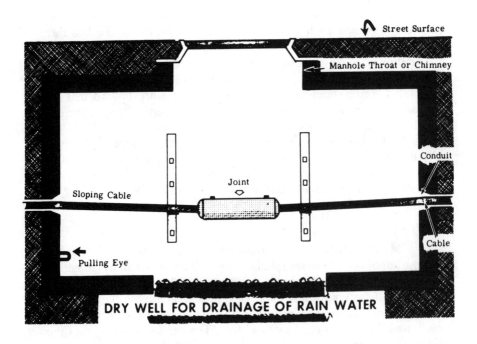

Fig. 4–7 Typical manhole with dry well.

waterfront in cities, for example, manholes are constructed of water-proof concrete, and sometimes also painted with waterproof paint for extra protection.

Manholes suitable for the installation of transformers (and other equipment) are usually constructed of reinforced concrete, but may have two chimneys or throats, one situated at each end of the manhole to provide adequate ventilation for the units installed therein.

Cable Installation

Cables may be installed directly in the ground in open fields or under suburban and rural roads. They may be drawn into ducts or installed in pipes in more or less densely populated urban and suburban areas, or laid in troughs in special cases such as under bridge structures or in tunnels (Fig. 4–8). The most desirable method of installation will depend on the voltage being carried, kind of cable, and the area in which it is installed.

Transmission Cable

Extreme care should be exercised when installing high-voltage cables, particularly in the case of gas- and oil-filled pressure types, and especially when pulling them in a duct or pipe. The stresses set up in the cables during this operation may cause damage to the conductors, the insulation, and the gas or oil paths. Outer armor wires, usually spiraled about a cable for protection in handling, may tighten about a cable so as to damage the insulation, and cut off the flow of gas or oil in that type cable. Some of the lengths of gas and oil cables pulled in at one time may measure in the thousands of feet. Dynamometers, instruments designed to measure tension, are frequently employed during the pulling process to ascertain that allowable pulling stresses are not exceeded (see Fig. 4–9).

Cables are spliced where necessary: in straight-type joints, in semistop-joints or in stop-joints, described previously. Attention is given to making the oil or gas paths continuous, with valved bypasses provided at semistop- and stop-joints. Manholes or protective concrete boxes are usually provided to contain the joints, although the straight-type joints are sometimes buried directly in the ground.

The oil or gas paths in hollow-type cables and the pipes in pipe-type cables are cleaned by circulating fresh, clean, and degasified oil free from moisture, then by applying a high degree of vacuum to extract practically all air or gas remaining in them. After testing to ascertain that contaminants and ionizable air have been removed, air-,

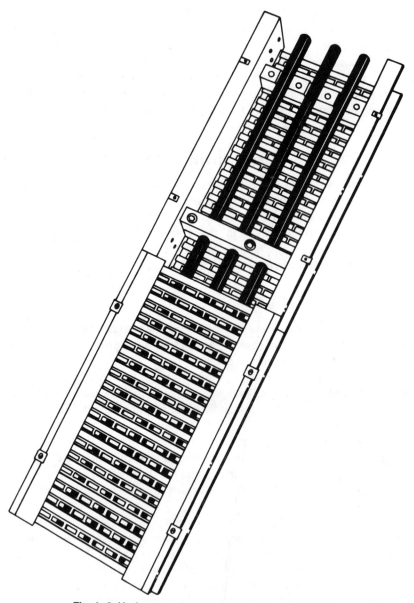

Fig. 4–8 Underground transmission cables installed in troughs.

contaminant-, and moisture-free oil or gas is introduced into the cable; bleed points along the cable allow checking to see that the cables are completely filled with insulating oil or gas.

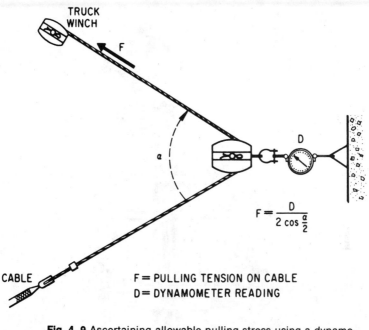

$$F = \frac{D}{2 \cos \frac{\alpha}{2}}$$

F = PULLING TENSION ON CABLE
D = DYNAMOMETER READING

Fig. 4–9 Ascertaining allowable pulling stress using a dynamometer.

Buried Distribution Cable

In installing such cable, care should be exercised to keep it from being damaged, especially avoiding dragging it over sharp stones or objects, or making sharp bends in it. In some cases, it may be desirable to place a layer of sand on the bottom of the trench as a precautionary measure; in some special cases, thermal sand may be placed to prevent excessive heating of the cable when electrically loaded. Cables may be laid on the ground adjacent to the trench and gently slid or placed into the trench; or, reels may be mounted on suitable trailers and the cable reeled off into the trench as the trailer is moved over the trench or parallel to it; or the cable may be pulled into the trench, particularly where shoring may be involved beneath the braces holding the shoring in place (Fig. 4–10).

In many instances, specifications call for laying cable (and other utility facilities) randomly at the bottom of the trench. At times, specifications call for minimum separation between the several facilities, not only on the same (horizontal) plane, but vertically as well; for example, secondary cables, or water pipes may be installed 6 or more inches above the primary cables (see Fig. 1–4). Here, one set of cables is

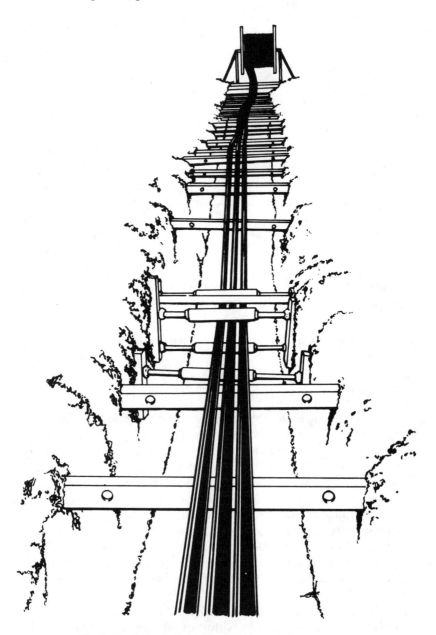

Fig. 4–10 Method of installing underground transmission cables buried directly in the ground.

installed, earth or sand is refilled into the trench to the proper specified depth, by machine, by hand, or both, and the other cables or facilities are installed; this may be repeated to some other depth, depending on specifications. Improved practices tend to place all the cables and facilities on one level, maintaining the specified spacings horizontally, even if a wider trench may be necessary.

Great care in screening out sharp rocks and other debris should be exercised in back-filling the trench so as not to damage the cable being covered. The dirt should be tamped down, but not packed too solidly. When the level of the next cable or facility is reached, care should be taken in leveling off the earth and smoothing the bed to receive the next cable or facility. This procedure is repeated for other installations until the trench is completely back-filled. In some cases, a plank may be installed at a level above the cables, to act as a protecting buffer when digging takes place in that area.

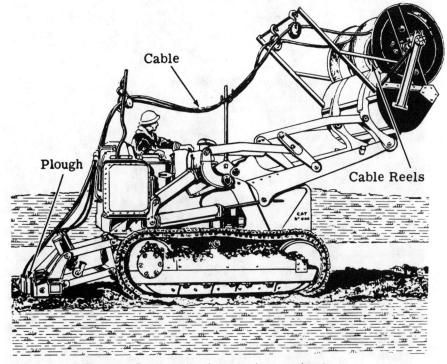

Fig. 4-11 Plowing cable for an underground system.

Some slack should always be left in the cable when it is installed so that, if it should be necessary to cut out a piece of the defective cable at the point of fault, it will be possible to repair the cable by means of a splice, without having to insert another piece or replace a part of the cable.

Scrap pieces of cable or pipe, and other metallic junk, such as nails, broken tools, beverage and other cans, etc., should be carefully removed from the trench and surrounding areas, since they may give false indications of the actual positions of the facilities installed.

Where the cable may be plowed into the ground, the plowing and burying of the cable may be done in one operation, and the sod pressed back in place after the plow has passed (Fig. 4–11). Where street crossings or driveways are encountered, it may prove practical to install

Fig. 4-12 Earth-boring machine.

conduits underneath them, threading the cable into them and laying the remainder in the ground or plowing into it.

Several means may be used to install these conduits without disturbing the surface of the ground. The conduit, usually a steel pipe, may be jacked through the soil for a short run. It may also be jetted hydraulically or tunneled or burrowed where soil conditions allow. Another method employs an auger or boring machine, working horizontally, which bores a hole into which a rigid or flexible steel or plastic conduit may be pushed (Fig. 4–12).

An underground piercing tool is available that enables cables to be run, and conduit, hoses, or pipes to be installed underground quickly, neatly, and without costly trenching, back-filling, or repaving. It is possible to tunnel without disturbing lawns, shrubs, sidewalks, streets, highways, or railroad tracks. Small starting and terminal trenches are all the digging that is needed (Fig. 4–13). It operates on compressed air, to produce smoothly cased tunnels of 3¾ inches to 5⅞ inches in diameter, using slip-on collars. Average speed varies according to soil composition and density. It tunnels through sandy soils, clay, or shale. It tunnels unaided and emerges "on target" as much as 100 feet or more away. In certain applications, copper or plastic tubing can be used as an air line, to save the time and effort of fishing or pushing the tubing through the hole.

Fig. 4–13 Underground-piercing tool.

The choice of method, again, depends on the particular circumstances surrounding the installation. In some cases, the conduits are installed in trenches, and reinforced with concrete before the trench is back-filled and paving restored. Cables are spliced where necessary, and the splices are buried directly in the ground. Similar procedures apply to the installation of services, street lighting, and other similar facilities.

Equipment Installation

Augers are used to drill holes in the ground adjacent to cables installed in trenches or plowed in the ground. These holes usually are used to construct the receptacles or vaults to contain transformers or other equipment, as mentioned earlier; they may also be used in carrying cable takeoffs to padmounted transformers and equipment. Where circular receptacles are installed to house underground transformers, or

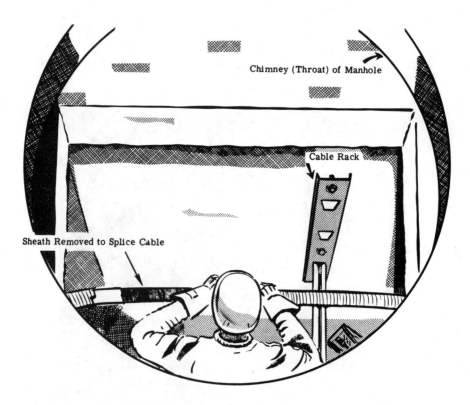

Fig. 4–14 Splicing a cable in a manhole.

where transformers or other equipment are to be buried directly in the ground, the diameter of the auger may be slightly larger than that of the receptacle or transformer, or other equipment, enabling them to slip easily into the hole. Backhoes and other digging equipment may be used in excavation, and back-filling blades to cover the excavation, after receptacles, vaults, transformers, and equipment directly buried in the ground are installed.

Pads may be of concrete, precast or poured in place, either at ground level, or below the ground a short distance (for low-profile enclosures) to accommodate the desired installation. More recently, these pads have been made of prefabricated plastic materials.

Round receptacles for transformers and other equipment may be made of plastic or concrete; often these may be a section of large-diameter standard concrete pipe used for water or sewer mains.

Where manholes or underground vaults are specified, these may be prefabricated and installed in excavations made by machines or by hand (Fig. 4–14), or they may be of reinforced concrete poured in place. All of these enclosures may contain transformers, switches, fuses, and other equipment, as described in preceding chapters.

Coordination of Utilities

Installing a number of utility facilities in the same trench may contribute greatly to the economy of underground systems, but to be successful, a great deal of coordination among the several utilities is necessary. Such coordination among the utility companies begins in the planning stages and continues through the design and actual construction stages, and includes scheduling the delivery of material to the job site, having the required personnel and equipment available, securing the necessary permits, preparing the job site, getting the local builders who may be developing new areas to demarcate property lines, and having municipal and other authorities designate curbs, catch basis, and other associated facilities.

Coordination of the differing construction standards of the several utilities must also be made; the determination of the specification for minimum vertical separation, for example, cannot only be time consuming, but adds substantially to the cost of such projects. Except where a single contractor is permitted to do the work for all the utilities involved, a turn-key operation, the coordination of labor practices of the several organizations involved adds to the complexities. Experience indicates that the problems associated with such joint installations, although capable of solutions, are administratively among the most complex and difficult.

Ducts and Manholes

Where cables are installed in underground ducts and manholes, it is first necessary to choose the duct to be used (where several ducts may exist) in the manhole. Unnecessary crossings of cables in the manhole should be avoided, as their obstructing other empty ducts should also be. Attention should be given to placing them so that work on them (pulling, splicing, etc.) may be done with adequate working space for the workmen (Fig. 4–15). Also, provisions should be made for the proper racking of cables and joints, and the proper separation of them, so that work on any one of them in the future may be performed safely (Fig. 4–16).

After the duct has been selected, it must be cleaned, and a pulling line must be installed. This may be done by pushing a brush attached to a series of short rods assembled on one another through the duct; when the brush reaches the next manhole, the rods are pulled through and disassembled, but a light manila line is attached to the last rod, so that when the last rod is removed, the line will be installed in the duct. This operation is sometimes accomplished by blowing the brush to which the manila line is attached through the duct by means of compressed air. The light manila line is then used to pull a heavier manila or steel rope for pulling the cable. Often, however, the pulling line is placed in the duct at the time of its installation.

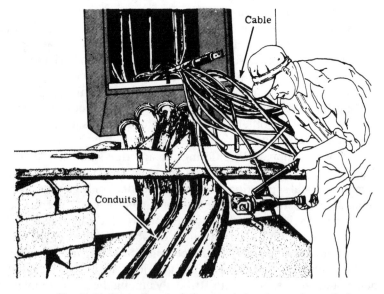

Fig. 4–15 Illustration depicting ample head room in manhole.

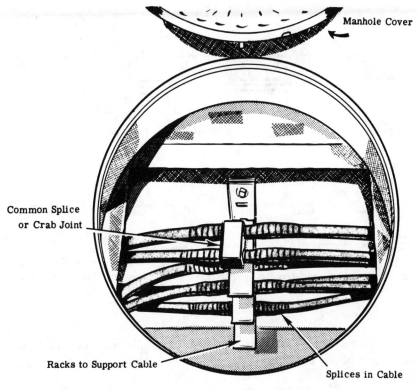

Common Splice
or Crab Joint

Racks to Support Cable

Splices in Cable

Fig. 4–16 Cables spliced and racked in a manhole.

Pulling the cable through the duct requires that the reel of cable be properly placed at the feeding end, and a winch, capstan, or truck at the pulling end. Several different ways of attaching the cable to the pulling line are shown (see Fig. 4–17). To protect the cable from injury during installation, the cable is usually greased while being installed. The feeding end of the duct is smoothed and it is good practice to pull the cable slowly.

The feeding end of the duct should be the end nearest which a bend or curve, if they exist, is located. Its effect in increasing the pulling tension will be less than if the curve is near the pulling end, since the tension due to the friction back of the curve will be smaller. The pulling operation, therefore, should be so arranged that the cable or cables are fed into the end nearest the sharpest and longest curves. (One exception is the case of risers connected to a relatively long horizontal duct; here the cable is fed downward through the riser, the weight of the cable tending to force it to the outside of the bend and eliminating the usual

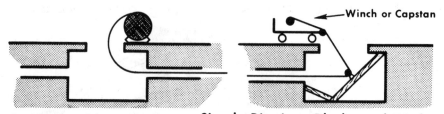

Feeding Cable into a Duct   Simple Rigging--Blocks and Wedges

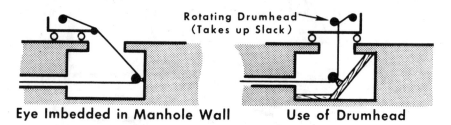

Eye Imbedded in Manhole Wall   Use of Drumhead

Fig. 4-17 Some methods of pulling cable through a duct.

effect of a bend in increasing the pulling tension.) It must be noted that the length of the curvature in a duct as well as its radius affects the cable-pulling tension.

Whether a cable or cables of a certain size can be pulled without damage into a given size duct may be determined in one of two ways. One way is to pull a mandrel approximately 24 inches long and ¼ inch greater in diameter than the cable, or cables, to be pulled; this represents a limiting condition. In cases in which the duct run contains unusual bends or curves, it may be well to pull through it a test section of cable, preferably junk or scrap cable, of the same or slightly larger diameter than that of the cable or cables to be permanently installed.

The location of cables in manholes is largely determined by the ducts they occupy. High-voltage transmission cables are usually placed at the bottom, out of the way where damage to them is less likely. Primary cables, secondary cables, and service cables are located successively above; the more accessible positions of the secondary cables are desirable, since they are usually worked upon more frequently than any of the others.

Where a large number of cables enters a manhole, the cable entrances to the manhole should be staggered and spacing should be increased. Fanning out duct runs in this manner, as they approach the manhole, simplifies training of the cables in the manhole.

Sections of cables installed in underground ducts are connected in the manhole to form a continuous length; the connection is called a "straight" joint or splice. It is possible to connect more than two cables together, and these are known as three-way, four-way, etc., splices. The method of making such splices is the same as was described for buried cables.

Cables should be racked in manholes so that they may expand and contract without damaging the sheath or splice. This is done by providing a large reverse curve, consisting of one or two large-radius bends, in the cable passing through the manhole. Cables and joints should be mounted on racks with porcelain insulator saddles so that the weight of the cable is supported by the racks and not hang from the splices, tending to pull them apart.

For ready accessibility, one cable per rack is desirable. This makes it possible to work on or remove the cable without disturbing the other cables. Two cables on a rack are often necessary and reasonably accessible, but more than two makes it very difficult to work on the cable adjacent to the wall.

From a reliability viewpoint, a separate rack should be provided for each cable, unless more than one cable is installed in one duct; in which case, all the cables in the same duct may be placed together on the same rack. This practice minimizes the danger of communicating trouble from one cable to another.

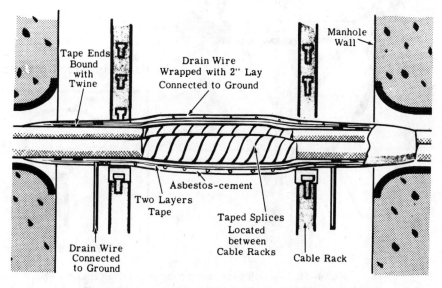

Fig. 4–18 Arcproofing single-conductor cables in a manhole.

Cable and joints should not be placed directly under the manhole opening because of the hazard from falling objects. If such an arrangement cannot be avoided, a shield should be interposed as a protection.

Where more than one cable passes through a manhole, it is sometimes desirable to fireproof (or arcproof) the cables and splices, to prevent spread of damage to other cables, should a fire or explosion occur from a failure or in the event gases in the manhole become ignited. The fireproofing usually consists of a layer of special cement approximately ½ inch thick, smoothed over the cables and splices; in some cases, particularly where a metallic sheath may be involved, a soft-drawn copper wire mesh tape is placed around the cables and splices underneath the special cement, and is subsequently connected to ground (Fig. 4–18).

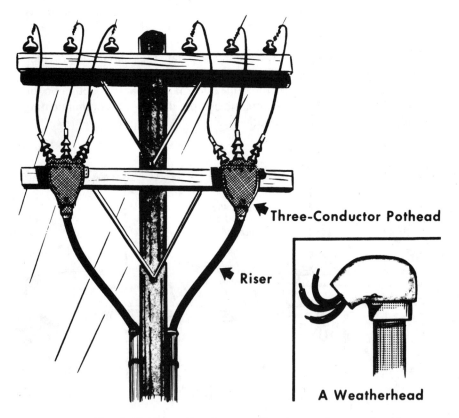

Three-Conductor Pothead

Riser

A Weatherhead

Fig. 4–19 Two potheads connecting two underground cable lines with two overhead lines.

Risers and Potheads

In many instances, underground cables are connected to overhead lines. To make this connection, the cable is led up to the side of the pole through a curved length of pipe and is terminated in a pothead; the whole assembly is known as a riser. For low-voltage (secondary or service) cables, a simpler weatherhead is used in place of the pothead (Fig. 4–19).

The pothead provides a weatherproof porcelain-encased terminal for each of the cable conductors to which the overhead conductors are connected. These terminals have petticoats to shed rain, and increase the length of the path between the live exposed overhead conduc-

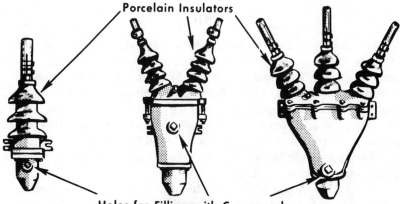

Porcelain Insulators

Holes for Filling with Compound

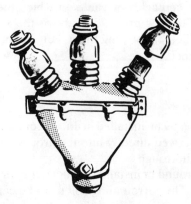

Fig. 4–20 Various types of potheads.

tor and the case of the pothead, or other metallic parts of the riser. The pothead body is filled with a liquid-insulating compound which cools into a solid. Potheads may be designed for one, two, or three conductors, and may be designed so that overhead conductors, terminating in an insulated cap, which fits over the underground terminals, may be readily disconnected. Such "disconnecting" potheads permit the opening of the line and are useful in locating trouble and provide a means of restoring service to a partly faulted circuit by transferring the supply to an adjoining circuit (Fig. 4–20).

Cable sheaths are attached to potheads by clamping devices, or by wiped joints to lead-sheathed cables. Where plastic-sheathed cables are involved, potheads are often not employed, but insulation is built up about the ends of the cables, leaving the conductors exposed, to which terminals of some kind are attached.

Safety

The normal safety precautions taken on similar construction projects should be observed. Warning signs and flags, barriers, cones and barricades, flares and bombs for nighttime, and flagmen and traffic directors, where necessary, should all be employed where required. Equipment should be operated according to safe operating practices and maintained in good operating condition. Workers should follow appropriate safety rules and practices; tools should be handled in the manner and for the purpose for which they were designed and should be maintained properly and regularly.

Cables should have some identification; these may be in the form of colored plastic tapes, or metallic tags attached to the cable, or both. Similar identification should be applied to transformers and other equipment and the receptacles or vaults in which they are contained. Markers on the surface, or protruding above the surface, should be installed not only to help in locating them, but also to warn the general public of their existence.

Review

- Underground cables may be installed in ducts (conduits) or pipe, may be laid in a trench, or plowed directly into the ground; in some instances, they may be placed in troughs.
- When buried in the ground or installed in ducts, they are placed at depths below the frost line. The surrounding soil must be capable of adequate heat dissipation to prevent overheating and failure of the cable. To

prevent hot spots, spare ducts may be provided and left vacant, or special earth or "thermal" sand may replace the soil in that particular area (Fig. 4–6).

- Duct sections are laid in tiers and properly spaced; popular duct sizes are 3, 3½, 4, and 5 inches in diameter. Large-radius curves may be formed by short straight sections connected by couplings or joints; the angle between adjacent sections is generally limited to 10°. The duct bank may be encased in concrete or buried in well-tamped earth.
- For short runs, ducts made of steel pipe may be jacked, jetted hydraulically, or tunneled through the earth.
- In pulling cable, the feeding end of the duct should be the end nearest which a bend or curve is located. Its effect in increasing the pulling tension will be less than if the curve is near the pulling end, since the tension due to friction back of the curve will be smaller. It must be noted that the length of the curvature in a duct, as well as its radius, affects the cable-pulling tension.
- To assure that allowable pulling stresses are not exceeded, dynamometers are often employed while pulling cable (Fig. 4–9).
- Scrap pieces of pipe, cable and other metallic junk, such as nails, broken tools, beverage cans, and other items, should be carefully removed from a trench and its surrounding areas, since they may give false indications of the actual positions of the facilities installed.
- Some slack should be left in the cables when installed so that, if necessary to cut out a small piece at the point of fault, there will be enough to make repairs by means of a splice, rather than replace or insert a new piece in the section of cable.
- Cables are spliced, racked, tested, and grouped in manholes. Cables must be racked so that the sheath can expand or contract without cracking. This is done by providing a large reverse curve, consisting of one or two large-radius bends, in the cable passing through the manhole. They must be shaped and mounted carefully so that splices will be supported without strain (Fig. 4–16).
- Where more than one cable passes through a manhole, it is sometimes desirable to fireproof (or arcproof) the cables and splices, to prevent spread of damage to other cables, should a fire or explosion occur from a failure or in the event gases in the manhole become ignited (Fig. 4–18).

Study Questions

1. How may underground cables be installed?
2. What precautions should be used in installing underground cables?

3. What precautions should be used in installing cables with other utilities in the same trench?
4. What measures are sometimes taken to protect cables while digging in their vicinity?
5. Why should slack always be left in the cable when installed?
6. Why should scrap pieces of metallic objects be removed from trenches and surrounding areas when back-filling?
7. How may conduits be installed in the ground? Of what materials may they be made?
8. What determines the size and shape of a manhole?
9. Why are cables racked and arcproofed in manholes?
10. How are underground cables identified?

5

maintenance and operation considerations

When it becomes necessary to work on an existing underground system, particularly where its components may be buried directly in the ground, additional precautions should be taken. Such work can include additions to such facilities, replacement because of inadequacy or defect, and repair because of damage or failure.

Locating Underground Facilities

Before work is undertaken on buried underground facilities, maps should be consulted and field markers should be checked to locate the facilities on which work is to be done. Complete reliance on these, however, should not be had, as the maps could be in error and field markers tampered with. The actual presence of the facilities should be confirmed by means of locating devices that can determine the position and depth of metallic objects (Fig. 5–1).

These instruments, which sweep over the ground much like mine detectors, operate on the same principle. A magnetic field, usually created by a battery, sweeps the area being probed and produces a steady sound picked up by earphones. When the magnetic field intersects a metallic object, a small voltage is induced in that object, which will cause a small current to be set up in the object, producing another magnetic field that will tend to oppose the magnetic field put out by the metal detector and that will change the sound produced, usually rather

Fig. 5–1 Cable locator.

sharply. This may be heard as a "clicking" sound in the earphones. Sometimes the earphones are replaced by a voltmeter, which will give the same indications by a swing of its needle.

Excavation

After determining and confirming the location of facilities, a test pit should be carefully dug by hand, until the facilities are exposed and further identified by tags or markers on the cable or equipment. Excava-

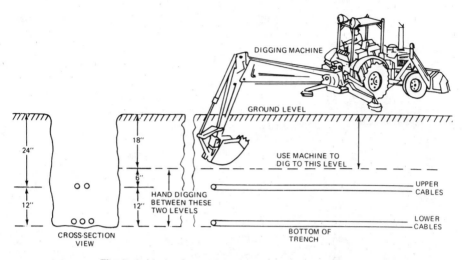

Fig. 5-2 Limit of machine digging to within 6 inches of cables first encountered.

tion can then proceed further, using machines and mechanized tools, such as backhoes and jackhammers, if conditions warrant. Caution should be used and excavation by such means stopped when it reaches a depth of approximately 6 inches from the facilities to be exposed; for example, if the first facilities to be encountered are buried at a depth of 24 inches, such mechanized digging may be done to a maximum of about 18 inches. Below this level, digging should be done by hand, using hand tools equipped with wooden or other nonconducting handles and dry work gloves (Fig. 5-2).

Where excavating is done to expose electric facilities, particularly primary cables, rubber gloves and sleeves should be worn as well as rubber boots, especially in wet areas or where water may exist. Where ground water is encountered in the initial digging, a sump hole may be dug at a distance laterally from the facilities of at least 3 feet for use with pumping equipment.

Before entering a manhole or underground vault, even momentarily, it should be tested for combustible or asphyxiating gases, and then ventilated thoroughly, using power blowers when necessary; it should be kept ventilated as long as work continues in or near it (Fig. 5-3).

Work on Cables

Before working on cables, they should be properly identified, and protected by barriers and other devices of sufficient dielectric strength to safeguard personnel working in the vicinity of energized

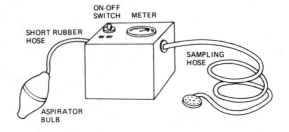

Fig. 5-3A Gas indicator.

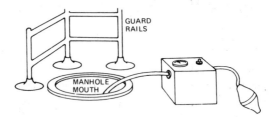

Fig. 5-3B Testing for gas.

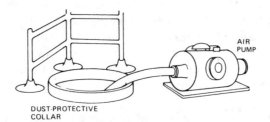

Fig. 5-3C Ventilating manhole by pump.

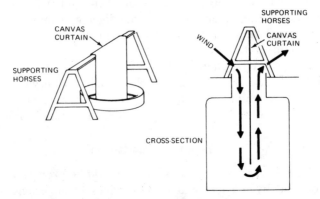

Fig. 5-3D Natural ventilation of manhole using wind.

cables and cable accessories, such as arcproofing, bonds to ground and between cables, etc. These devices may consist of rubber or plastic blankets and preformed shapes to fit over cables, splices, and other equipment; these should be installed by qualified personnel, wearing rubber protective devices mentioned earlier. Barriers made of plastic or other insulating material, and which should be flameproof as well, should be placed strategically to protect workers from possible flame and arcs from electric failures, and from flying debris.

Transmission Cables

While solid-type cables require relatively little maintenance and are comparatively easy to replace or repair, oil- and gas-filled cables present much greater difficulties. Oil or gas leaks occasionally occur and these must be found and repaired, generally without deenergizing the cable.

Small leaks may be detected by the drop in oil or gas pressure indicated at the point where oil or gas sources are fed into the cable, usually at one of the terminals. Further pressure checks at the semistop-joints and stop-joints will gradually narrow the leak location to a section between two of these joints; inspection of the cables (where possible) and splices between them will usually suffice to find the leak. In many cases, the small leak may be allowed to flow until telltale oil puddles or surface indication of a gas leak reveal the location. Repairs can be accomplished, without deenergizing the feeder, by small patches on the sheath or pipe.

Larger leaks are more readily found, generally by field inspection along the route of the line. The cable sheath or pipe can be repaired in place by deenergizing the feeder and shutting off the oil or gas flow between two semistop- or stop-joints. After the repairs to the cable are made, the sections will have to be flushed, with oil or gas from which contaminants and moisture have been removed, and then refilled under a vacuum.

Where oil-filled cables have to be pieced out or replaced, from failure or whatever reason, it is necessary to seal off the flow of oil on both sides of the section on which work is to be performed. This is done by freezing an oil slug from the outside of the cable or pipe by pouring liquid nitrogen until there is assurance the oil flow has stopped. These low temperatures are maintained by encasing the cable or pipe in ice and by continued dripping of liquid nitrogen. The cable or pipe may then be cut, cables replaced, repaired, or rerouted, and in the case of pipe cables, the pipe assembly welded together again. Care is taken to reestablish the protective covering. Before reenergization, it is necessary not only to replace the oil in the affected section, but to ascertain that all of the oil in the system is free from air, moisture, and other contaminants, a time-consuming and expensive process.

The freezing method consists of a split lead sleeve, about 2 feet in length, with two stand-pipes (Fig. 5–4). The sleeve is opened sufficiently to pass around the cable or pipe. The gap is then closed and sealed along the longitudinal length with solder. The ends are then sealed to the cable jacket or pipe by the application of rubber tapes and reinforcing tapes such as hessian. The whole of the sleeve and the stand-pipes are then insulated with asbestos lagging either in tape or rope form. Liquid nitrogen is poured into the freezing sleeve, via a funnel, to one of the stand-pipes; the other acting as a vent for the exhaust of the nitrogen vapor. Experience has shown that the time required to provide a solid blockage in a cable of approximately 2½ inches outside diameter is 30 minutes and for cables of about 4 inches in diameter, 1 hour.

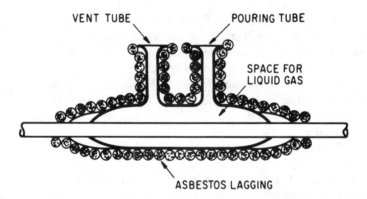

Fig. 5–4 Freezing a section of an oil-filled cable to isolate a leak.

For gas-filled cables, replacement is much simpler. The gas flow is valved off at the semistop-joints or stop-joints on both sides of the affected section, the section of cable replaced and respliced, and the procedure for flushing and refilling under vacuum repeated as described earlier for repair of oil or gas leaks. In repairing gas-filled cables, the gas in one of the sections is completely replaced, and no operation similar to the oil freezing is required.

Solid-type cables are handled in the same manner as primary distribution cables, described below.

After all these mechanical, thermal, and dielectric barriers and devices have been installed, yet another precaution is taken before working on primary cables that are considered to be deenergized. This employs a device containing a spear or spiker (Fig. 5–5) which is attached to the cable (or splice) and connected to a ground or neutral; it is operated remotely, either by a long insulated wooden or plastic stick, or hydraulically, from behind a barrier. The device punctures the cable, making contact with the conductor. A high-voltage tester, or voltmeter (for secondary cables), is connected between the spear or spiker and the neutral conductor or ground; these should be visible to the workers behind the protective barrier a safe distance away.

Fig. 5–5 Cable spiker.

If the cable is energized, some arcing and flame may occur, and the device may even be destroyed, but the cable is deenergized by the protective fuses or breakers actuated by the short circuit applied by the device; this should be ascertained before any other work is done. If nothing occurs, and a check with the voltage tester or voltmeter indicates the cable is deenergized, work may proceed as planned.

There may be instances, however, where, because of a high-resistance ground or open circuit, and the spear or spiker remaining energized, nothing still happens; a check with the voltage tester or voltmeter should reveal whether or not the conductor is still energized, and other operations will be necessary to deenergize the conductor, which will now need repair.

Before proceeding to work on deenergized cable (or equipment), still another precaution is taken. The cable is first handled by the workers wearing protective devices, and suitable grounds are placed on both sides of the cable (or equipment), if possible, on which work is to be done (Fig. 5-6). The cable conductor may now be exposed.

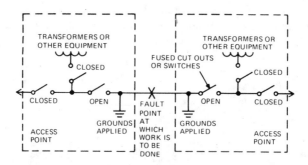

Fig. 5-6 Schematic one-line diagram showing application of protective grounds on both sides of point on cables on which work is to be done.

Secondary Distribution Cables

In general, underground cables are almost always deenergized before work is done on them. In some cases, however, with proper safeguards, work may be done on secondary cables while energized.

Work on Transformers and Equipment

Transformers installed in vaults or on pads above ground may be readily inspected and replaced while the primary conductors may be energized. With the primary conductors disconnected from the transformers, by pulling (with a long insulated stick) the insulated elbows, separating the cables from the transformers, and the secondary cables disconnected from the transformers, insulated protective devices are placed to cover any energized portions and terminals of both primary and secondary cables (Fig. 5-7). Suitable barriers are placed to keep personnel at a safe distance while working on the transformers.

Transformers installed below grade in semiburied vaults, in receptacles and vaults completely below ground, or buried directly in the ground should be deenergized, including the cables connected to them, when it is necessary to inspect, maintain, repair, or replace them. Inspection may include cover bolts, signs of corrosion, and any effects of insecticides and fertilizers on cables and tanks, signs of overheating,

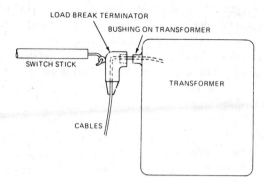

LOAD BREAK TERMINATOR
BUSHING ON TRANSFORMER
SWITCH STICK
TRANSFORMER
CABLES

Fig. 5-7 Disconnecting primary cable from transformer by pulling load-break terminator using insulated switch stick.

ascertaining that cables are not lying against transformer tanks, and any other signs of incipient troubles. In addition to inspection, other maintenance may include painting of the tanks, replacement of bushings, gaskets, anodes for cathodic protection, changing of taps, and tightening connections, and insulting or replacing neutral conductors and grounds. Often, almost all of these may be done, whether entirely necessary or not, as preventive maintenance, once the transformer is exposed. See page 38 for PCB precautions.

When work is done to expose such transformers (below grade, semiburied, or direct buried), the same procedures for excavating and working should be followed as were outlined previously for cable installations (see Fig. 5–2). Rubber gloves and sleeves should be worn by personnel, using wooden-handled and insulated hand tools for excavating below the uppermost clear depth layer (usually 24 inches), in a similar manner as in exposing primary cables.

Fuses associated with primary laterals or transformers are usually installed in vaults or receptacles, so that they may be readily replaced without affecting the operation of the transformers. Similarly, the handles that enable the reclosing of the secondary breakers on CSP transformers, may be operated safely by means of a long insulated stick.

Switches installed in similar enclosures may also be operated safely by means of a long insulated stick. The replacement and maintenance of fuse cutouts and switches generally follow the same procedures as for transformers.

Electrolysis

Stray direct currents, resulting from railroad return circuits, from galvanic action between dissimilar metals, and from other causes, may affect underground installations, particularly in areas where the soil may be wet or damp. Two (or more) metallic structures, immersed in the chemical solutions present in the earth, create an action, called electrolysis, causing metal from one structure to flow and deposit itself upon the other structure. The direction of this flow depends on the relative voltages existing between the two structures, the flow being from the one of higher voltage to the one of lower voltage.

Where the higher-voltage metallic structure is the steel tank of a transformer (or other underground equipment), metal will be drawn away from the tank, eventually wearing it away and causing failure. While insulating paints are of some usefulness, a more positive method is to connect to the steel tank a piece of another metal, usually magnesium, which will produce an even higher voltage than the steel tank, will cause current, and metal, to flow from it, rather than the steel tank. This piece of metal, usually called an anode, will sacrifice itself to protect the steel tank of the transformer. While this electrolytic action will be more pronounced on cables and transformers buried directly in the ground, it will also affect those installed in ducts and manholes.

These anodes should be inspected regularly, and replaced when necessary. In some cases, where other work nearby may make available the sacrificial anodes used for cathodic protection against corrosion, they may be replaced without deenergizing the transformer.

Restoration of Service

When a fault occurs which may interrupt all or a portion of a primary circuit, it is usually desirable to restore service to as much of the affected circuit as possible, before finding and repairing the fault.

Radial Circuits

In a radial circuit or feeder, interruptions may occur which affect different portions of the circuit. A failure in secondary mains may blow the fuse protecting the transformer which supplies it (or open the secondary breakers of a CSP transformer). Should a fault occur in a transformer (and the fuses not blow), or in the cables comprising the lateral takeoff from the feeder main, the line fuse protecting the lateral should blow, confining interruptions to that portion of the circuit.

Should the line fuse fail to blow, or a fault develop in the feeder main, the entire feeder will become deenergized, with the circuit breaker opening at the station. If the circuit has emergency ties to adjacent circuits, the circuit is sectionalized, much as described in the procedures for open-loop circuits, and the unfaulted portions of the circuit energized through these emergency ties to the adjacent circuits (Fig. 5–8).

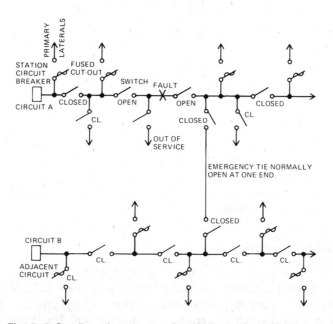

Fig. 5-8 One-line diagram showing method of sectionalizing faulted circuit and reenergizing unfaulted section from adjacent circuit.

Where such emergency ties do not exist, the circuit may be sectionalized, as described earlier, and the circuit energized up to the section in fault. If the fault is in a lateral, it may be disconnected and the feeder restored to service; only service to the lateral will be affected. If the fault is on the feeder main, the portion of the circuit beyond the fault will be affected.

If practical, whether on the main portion of the feeder or on a lateral, a temporary jumper above ground may be installed to bypass the defective section of cable, and service restored. If not practical, interruption to those portions of the circuit that may be affected, will continue until repairs are completed.

Duplicate Primary Supply

Where duplicate primary supply is provided, the deenergization of one of the feeders, the normal supply, may cause interruption to service. Restoration may be accomplished by switching from the normal source to the alternate source; this may be done automatically, in which case the interruption may be momentary or of short duration, or may be done manually with a longer interruption time (Fig. 5–9).

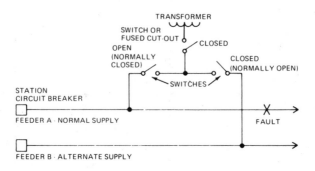

Fig. 5-9 One-line diagram showing method of energizing supply to transformer from alternate supply source, where duplicate supplies are provided.

Closed-Loop Circuit

In a closed-loop circuit, a fault in a section of the cable should automatically disconnect the faulted section at the breakers at both ends; however, there may be one or more transformers connected to the faulted section that will experience an interruption. These are usually connected to the cable through disconnecting devices which permit them to be disconnected from the portions of the cable in either direction away from the transformer. By opening the disconnect, or disconnects, associated with the faulted portion of the cable, and closing the breaker or breakers involved, service may be restored while the fault is located and repaired (Fig. 5–10).

Open-Loop Circuit

In an open-loop circuit, when a fault occurs the entire circuit or a portion of the circuit may be deenergized, depending on where the loop is normally open. Service may be restored by opening the loop on both sides of the fault, and closing the remainder of the loop at both ends. In determining the section in which the fault is located, the loop is opened approximately at midpoint and a test for ground is made in both directions; if a positive indication is not obtained, fuses may be replaced at both ends (if blown), and the fuse on the part containing the fault will blow. The process is repeated approximately halfway between the first test point and the end of the faulted part of the feeder; and again, if necessary, between the second test point and the end of the feeder, or the first test point, depending on which side the fault is indicated. This is repeated until the fault is finally located between two adjacent sectionalizing points; the faulted section is disconnected at both ends, and

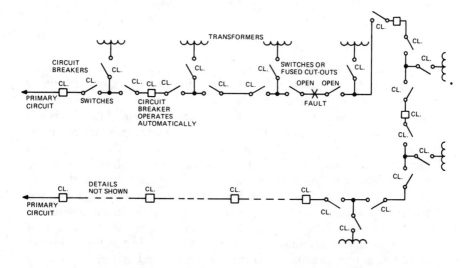

Fig. 5–10 One-line diagram showing method of reenergizing unfaulted portions of a closed-loop primary circuit.

the remaining parts of the feeder are energized from both ends of the loop (Fig. 5–11).

The test for grounds may be made with a megger, or with a simple battery and lamp or ammeter connected in series, and the terminals may be connected between the cable conductor and the neutral or

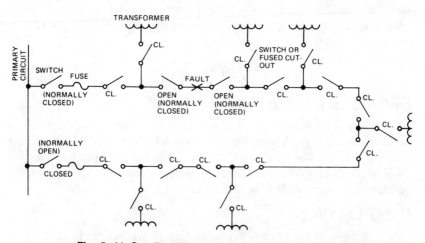

Fig. 5–11 One-line diagram showing method of reenergizing unfaulted portions of an open-loop primary circuit.

ground. Little or no current will flow in the good portion of the cable, while a relatively large current will flow in the defective portion.

Low Voltage Network

In a low-voltage network, the deenergization of one primary feeder supply will not interrupt service; the deenergization of two or more feeders may cause the entire network to become deenergized. Simply, when sufficient primary feeders are ascertained to be serviceable, by disconnecting any defective transformers, switches or equipment, if necessary, the network may be reenergized by the simultaneous closing of the feeder breakers at the station from which they emanate.

Although the size of the network is designed to be of sufficiently small capacity that the load picked up will not overload generators, transmission lines, substations or other sources, the instantaneous inrush, especially if the network has been deenergized for any length of time, may cause overload protective relays to trip the feeder circuit breakers; hence, in some instances, the relays are blocked temporarily to prevent their operation during startup. Also, the power supply to close circuit breakers should be checked to make sure it is adequate for positive operation of the number of circuit breakers required to be closed simultaneously.

A fault on a section of secondary mains will cause the fuses or limiters on either end of the section to blow and disconnect the section from the network; consumers on this section will be out of service until the section is replaced or the fault repaired. Should the fuses or limiters not blow, fault current will continue to flow until more remote fuses or limiters blow, or the secondary mains burn themselves clear at some points, to isolate the fault from the rest of the network (Fig. 5–12).

Fault Finding

Isolation of Faulted Section

The first step in locating a fault is to isolate it to the shortest practical section, preferably between two adjacent access points. This can be done by testing with a battery and voltmeter (or lamp), testing the cable in trouble, in both directions, at each successive access point, for open, short, or grounded circuits (Fig. 5–13).

Cable Locating

The next step in finding a fault on an underground cable is to determine the location of the cable in the ground (except where it may be in conduits and manholes, whose location is already known). This is done with metal detectors, mentioned previously.

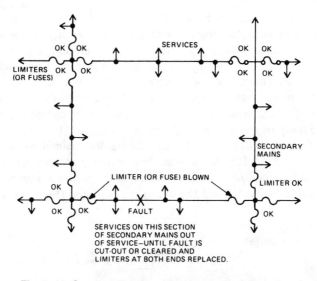

Fig. 5–12 One-line diagram showing how limiters isolate faulted section or secondary main, in low-voltage network.

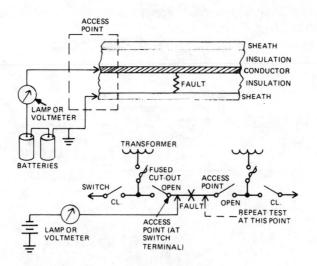

Fig. 5–13 Schematic diagram showing method of testing to isolate faulted section of cable.

Since the metal detector may locate other utilities or metallic substructures, it may be desirable to have the transmitter generate a magnetic field in the buried conductor, either by connecting the transmitter directly to the conductor at some convenient accessible point, or induce it in the conductor by a probe driven into the ground adjacent to the conductor at some point where the location of the conductor is known. The receiver locates the conductor by detecting and tracing this electromagnetic field (Fig. 5–14). As the conductor is approached, the volume of the signal tone will increase; when it is directly over the conductor, in some type (high frequency) detectors, the volume of the tone will be a maximum, while in others (low frequency), the volume will drop suddenly to a slight or "null" value (Fig. 5–15).

The depth of the conductor may be determined by holding the receiver at a 45° angle parallel to the line of the conductor and moving it away from the conductor at right angles until a new maximum signal or null point is obtained. Then the depth is calculated (Fig. 5–16).

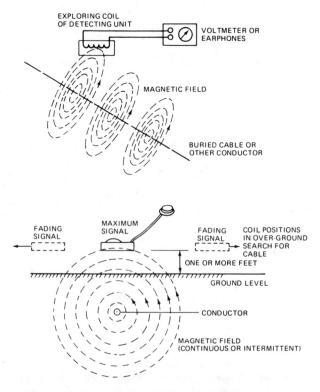

Fig. 5–14 Principle of metal detecting unit.

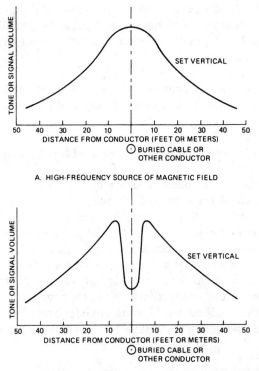

A. HIGH-FREQUENCY SOURCE OF MAGNETIC FIELD

B. LOW-FREQUENCY SOURCE OF MAGNETIC FIELD

Fig. 5–15 Variation in tone or signal volume with distance from conductor.

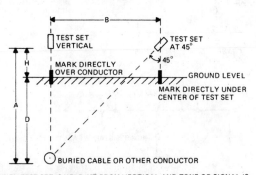

WHEN TEST SET IS HELD 45° FROM VERTICAL AND TONE OR SIGNAL IS MAXIMUM (OR MINIMUM FOR LOW-FREQUENCY SOURCE), A WILL EQUAL B. DEPTH OF CONDUCTOR, THEREFORE, WILL BE: D = B - H

Fig. 5–16 Determining depth of buried cable or other conductor.

Care should be exercised in locating the cable, since indications both as to location and depth may be in error, and especially if the cables contain shielding tapes, or if other utilities or underground metallic structures exist in the vicinity. Good practice dictates that a test pit be first dug by hand to uncover the cable in question and confirm the findings of the metal-locating instruments. Test methods are then applied to determine the location and nature of the fault.

Fault Breakdown

Should trouble be experienced in obtaining positive results, it may be that the nature of the fault will not permit sufficient test current to flow continuously, because of its high resistance or intermittent nature. If practical, the section of cable containing the fault is tested with a megger at one or both ends, to determine the resistance of the fault. Should this appear high or unstable, a high voltage (produced electronically in a "kenetron" set, but supplying a relatively small current) is applied to the cable, either at the station from which it emanates, or at one end of the cable in the field. This high voltage will burn down the fault into a more solid connection between the conductor and the neutral or ground; the small current flowing obviates any violent action from taking place and restricts damage to the cable to the point of fault (Fig. 5–17).

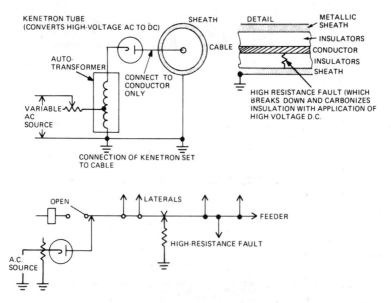

Fig. 5–17 Method of breaking-down fault on cable using high-voltage "kenetron" set.

Fault Location

Several means may be employed to pinpoint the location of the fault.

Tracing Current

A periodically interrupted signal or tracer current is applied to the conductor at one end, and the cable scanned at a convenient access point above ground with an exploring coil, which will pick up on a voltmeter (or in earphones) the periodic signal applied to the conductor. At the point of fault, this current flows to ground, so that no signal current (or only a very small fraction of it) will flow past it, and this will be observed on the voltmeter or in the earphones (Fig. 5–18).

Capacitance Method

A similar procedure, using the discharge of a capacitor applied to the conductor will be picked up as a "thump" by electronic devices similar to a radio, or in earphones. At the point of fault, the discharge will

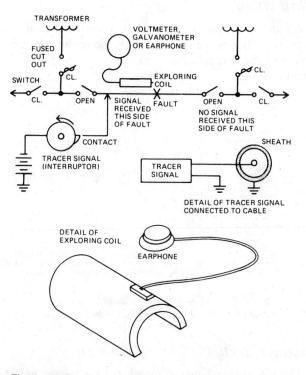

Fig. 5–18 One-line schematic diagram showing application of tracer current method for location of cable fault.

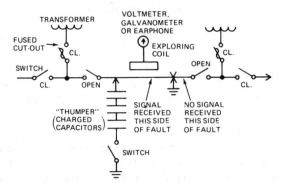

Fig. 5-19 One-line schematic diagram showing application of "thumper" method for location of cable fault.

produce a maximum signal, which will disappear beyond the point of fault (Fig. 5-19).

Traveling Wave

A radar-like system, applied at one end of the conductor, sends out a high-frequency wave which travels along the conductor; when it arrives at the fault, it is reflected and returns to the point of origin. The time consumed by the wave traveling to and from the fault is converted into distance, and the fault is thus located (Fig. 5-20).

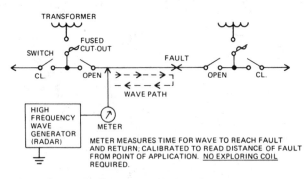

Fig. 5-20 One-line schematic diagram showing application of "radar" method of location of cable fault.

Wheatstone Bridge

The two parts of the section of cable, from the fault to each end of the section of cable, can be connected as two arms of a Wheatstone bridge, and the ratio of the resistance of each part can be determined; the ratio applied to the cable will determine the point of fault. This method may be more accurate than the others, and may be easy to apply where a second cable, paralleling the first, is available to complete the bridge circuit; otherwise, a wire must be run from one end of the conductor to the other (Fig. 5–21).

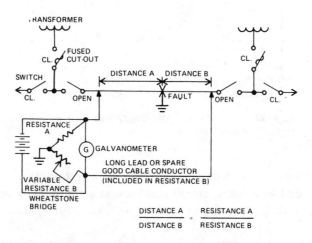

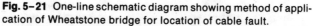

Fig. 5–21 One-line schematic diagram showing method of application of Wheatstone bridge for location of cable fault.

Crude Method

A cruder method, but often effective, connects one end of the cable conductor to one of the leads from the distributor of an automobile engine. When the engine is run, a high voltage is applied momentarily, as for the spark plug. An ordinary battery-operated portable radio will pick up the intermittent signal up to the point of fault, and no signal is heard beyond this point (Fig. 5–22).

Fault Indicators

To expedite the location of faults on underground systems where test points may not be readily available, such as those completely buried in the ground, a so-called fault indicator has been developed. This is essentially an inexpensive and "rough" overcurrent relay, with targets to indicate normal and fault operation. The device is installed at selected points along a circuit, usually at some (or all) transformer, switch, or tap points. The theory is that fault current flowing in a faulted circuit will operate these devices to the point nearest the fault, but will not operate

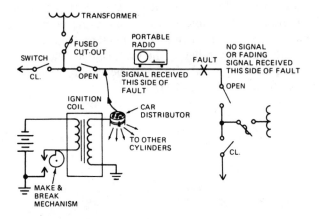

Fig. 5–22 One-line schematic diagram of "crude" method for location of cable fault.

beyond the point of fault where no fault current flows (Fig. 5–23). It is coordinated with fuses, circuit breakers, and reclosers, which may be connected in the circuit, so that these indicators will operate before the

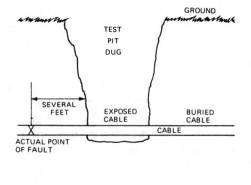

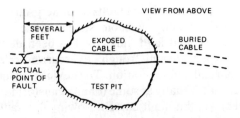

Fig. 5–23 Fault indicator and method of connection.

deenergizing devices operate. After the fault is cleared, these are reset for normal operation.

They may be installed without deenergizing the circuit. Basically, they consist of a current transformer, consisting of a split iron core and coil, to which the overcurrent target relay is connected. The split core can be mounted around the cable, and the relay installed remotely, say in a plastic box with hand cover at ground level, where it may be easily observed. They may also be used on cables installed in ducts, and on both single- and three-phase systems.

The first method described for locating a fault is often used on radial feeders, and on those supplying a low-voltage network. In these instances, the exploring coil is applied halfway out on the feeder, and the signal is observed; if the signal is detected the coil is then placed halfway between this point and the end of the circuit; if no signal is detected, then halfway between this point and the source of the circuit. The process is repeated until the section of cable containing the fault is found and on which the signal is observed at one end, but not on the other.

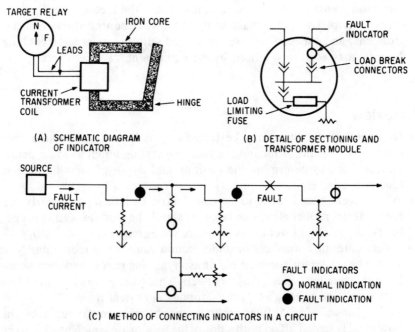

(A) SCHEMATIC DIAGRAM OF INDICATOR

(B) DETAIL OF SECTIONING AND TRANSFORMER MODULE

(C) METHOD OF CONNECTING INDICATORS IN A CIRCUIT

Fig. 5–24 Diagram showing possible actual location of fault from test hole dug.

Where the cable exists in conduits, it may be necessary to replace the entire section of cable. Where the cable is buried, caution should be exercised in digging at the point of fault so as not to disturb or damage other utilities that may also exist; it is equally important not to damage further the faulted cable. Although the fault may be located by the several means described above, it often may be as much as several feet from the point where the digging was done. To keep the amount of cable to be cut out and respliced within the slack available (as mentioned earlier), extreme care should be taken in removing the earth from the cable until the fault is reached (Fig. 5–24).

Conclusions

Obviously, it is impractical to attempt to detail all the possible situations and conditions that may prevail in installations in such diverse population centers and environments, under varying standards of operation, and in the different places where undergrounding of electric lines exists or is contemplated. Those described in this and preceding chapters are meant to be representative. Particular problems may require particular solutions, toward which, hopefully, the methods and procedures described here may make some worthwhile contributions. Special problems, and especially those associated with below-grade switching devices, may require solutions by the equipment manufacturers.

Review

- Underground facilities may be located by field markers, where they exist, or by means of locating devices, operating much as mine detectors, which can determine the position and depth of metallic objects (ducts, cables, etc.).
- Where excavating is done to expose electric facilities, particularly primary cables, rubber gloves and sleeves should be worn as well as rubber boots, especially in wet areas or where water may exist.
- Before entering a manhole or underground vault, even momentarily, it should be tested for combustible or asphyxiating gases, and then ventilated thoroughly, using power blowers where necessary; it should be kept ventilated as long as work continues in or near it.
- Where transmission oil-filled cables have to be pieced out or replaced, the flow of oil is sealed off on both sides of the section on which work is to be done. This is done by freezing an oil slug from the outside of the cable or

pipe by pouring liquid nitrogen over them until the oil ceases flowing, and continued thereafter until work is completed (Fig. 5–4).

- Before working on cables, and after all the mechanical, thermal, and dielectric barriers are installed, the cable or splice is penetrated by a grounded, remotely operated, spear or spike (Fig. 5–5). The device punctures the cable making contact with the conductor; some arcing or flame may occur, possibly destroying the device, if the cable is energized; a voltage tester indicates the cable is deenergized before work proceeds. In general, underground cables are almost always deenergized before work is done on them.

- In finding the fault on a section of cable, it is first necessary to isolate it to the shortest practical section, preferably between two adjacent access points; the cable location is then determined, whether in a manhole or, if buried, by means of metal detectors. Should trouble be experienced because of the high resistance of the fault, the fault may be burned down by the application of a short-time high voltage with a "kenetron" set (which supplies a relatively small current).

- Faults may be pinpointed by six different means:

  1. Tracing current: A periodically interrupted signal current applied to the conductor and picked up with an exploring coil at access points; beyond the fault, the signal disappears.

  2. Capacitance method: A similar procedure, using the discharge of a capacitor to produce a "thump"; at the point of fault, the discharge will produce a maximum signal, which will disappear beyond the point of fault.

  3. Traveling wave: A high-frequency wave is applied and travels along the conductor to the point of fault, where it is reflected and returns to the point of origin; the time consumed is then converted into distance from the point of wave application.

  4. Wheatstone bridge: Two parts of the section of cable, from the fault to each end, are connected as two arms of a Wheatstone bridge, and the ratio of the resistance of each part determined; the ratio applied to the cable will determine the point of fault.

  5. Crude method: One end of the cable conductor is connected to one of the leads from the distributor of an automobile engine. An ordinary portable radio will pick up the intermittent signal to the point of fault, and no signal beyond this point.

  6. Fault indicators: Devices, installed at convenient test points, and composed of inexpensive rough overcurrent relays, operate targets that indicate the direction of the fault; a "fault" target shows where fault current is measured, and a "normal" target shows at points beyond the fault.

Study Questions

1. How may underground cables be located before excavation?
2. What precautions should be taken in excavating for buried cables?
3. What special precaution should be taken before entering a manhole or underground vault?
4. What precautions should be taken before working on buried cables or equipment?
5. How may service be restored on primary distribution systems?
6. How may a circuit be sectionalized to determine fault location?
7. What steps are taken before pinpointing fault location in an underground cable?
8. What are several means of pinpointing fault locations?
9. What is a megger and where is it used?
10. What precautions should be taken in uncovering a fault in buried cables?

INDEX

INDEX

a-c, 1, 26; *see also* Alternating current
Alternating current, 1, 26; *see also* a-c
Aluminum, 6, 24
American Wire Gage, 25
Anode, 81–82
Appearance, 4, 6, 9, 24
Arc-proofing, 67–68, 77; *see also* Fire-
    proofing
Armor, 6–7, 55
Askarel, 38
Auger, 51, 61–63

Backhoe, 48–49, 63, 75
Bending Radius, 44, 66–67
Box, distribution, 45
Brick, 53
Bushing, 34–35, 37, 81

Cable, 4–6, 8, 10, 20–22, 24–34, 38–39,
    41–46, 48, 50–53, 55–62, 64–70, 74–
    75, 77–87, 89–90, 92–96
Cable locator, 74, 86, 91
Capacitance, 91
Cathodic protection, 81
CATV 7, 9, 21
Cerchi, Italy, 1
Charging current, 31
Circular mil, 25
Closed-loop, 15, 84–85
Concentric cable, 31–32
Concrete, 37, 43–44, 46, 48, 51–55, 63
Condenser, 31
Conductor, 1, 4–6, 8–9, 18, 24–27, 29,
    31–32, 34, 38–39, 44, 62, 70, 79–81,
    85, 88–89, 91, 93
Conduit, 4, 21, 40, 43, 48, 61, 87, 96;
    (*see also* Duct, trunk)
Coordination, 10, 63, 94
Copper, 5–6, 24–25, 61, 68
Corona, 26–27
Corrosion, 52, 80, 82
Cross-arm, 4
CSP (Completely Self Protected) trans-
    former, 37, 81–82

d-c, 1, 81; *see also* Direct current
Detector, metal, 73, 88
Digger, digging machine, 49, 51
"Dig-in", 8
Direct current, 1, 81; *see also* d-c
Distribution, 1, 4, 6, 10, 14, 19, 21, 24,
    29, 31, 41, 45, 52, 57, 78, 80
Duct, 4–7, 9, 20, 22, 24, 40–46, 48, 52–
    53, 55, 64–67, 82; *see also* Conduit,
    trunk
Dynamometer, 55, 57

Economy, economics, 4–6, 8–11, 15, 18–
    19, 21, 24, 40–41, 63
Edison, Thomas, 1
Electrolysis, electrolytic action, 8, 33,
    38, 52, 81–82
Epoxy, 38

Fault, 4, 8, 10, 13–15, 19, 28, 35, 37–39,
    44, 70, 82–84, 86–87, 90–96
Feeder, 6, 10–11, 13, 15, 17–18, 41, 45,
    82–83, 86
Fiber, 42, 53
Fire-proofing, 68, 77; *see also* Arc-
    proofing
Fuse, fusing, 14–15, 19, 37, 39, 63, 79,
    81–82, 84, 86, 94

Gas, 5, 7, 21, 25, 27–29, 46, 52, 55–56,
    76–78
Generating station, generator, 1, 3–4, 86
Great Barrington, Mass., 1
Ground, grounding, 10, 38–39, 68, 77,
    79–81, 85–86, 90–91

Hollow cable, 27–29, 55; *see also* Pirelli
    cable

Identification, 70, 73–75
Indicator, fault, 93–94
Insulation, insulator, 1, 5–6, 25–27, 29,
    31–32, 34, 37–38, 52, 55–56, 70, 77,
    80–82

Jackhammer, 51, 75
Joint, 29, 34–35, 55, 67–68, 70; *see also*
    Splice
Joint construction, 7, 9, 63

Kenetron, 90

Lead, 4–7, 10, 25, 31, 70, 78
Lightning, 8, 38
Lightning arrester, 37, 39–40
Limiter, 86–87
Locator, cable, 74, 86, 88, 90–91
Loops, 15–16, 19, 35, 37, 82, 84–85

Magnesium, 82
Manhole, 4–7, 20–21, 40–41, 43–46, 48,
    52–55, 62–64, 66–68, 75–76, 82, 87
Megger, 85, 90
Metal detector, 73, 88, 90

101

Network, low voltage, 17–18, 86; *see also* Secondary network
Neutral, 31–34, 38–39, 79, 81, 85, 90
New York City, 1
Nitrogen, 27, 77–78

Oil, 5–6, 25, 27–29, 31, 37, 39, 52, 55–56, 77–78
Oil-o-static cable, 29, 77; *see also* Pipe type cable
Open-loop, 15–16, 35, 82, 84
Overhead, 1–2, 4–5, 7–11, 13–14, 24–25, 29, 31, 37–40, 68–69
Ozone, 26

Pad, 80
Paper, 4–6, 10, 25, 31
Pilot wire, 16
Pipe, pipe type cable, 28–29, 31, 42, 44, 52, 55, 60, 61, 77–78; *see also* Oil-o-static cable
Pirelli cable, 28; *see also* Hollow cable
Planning, 13
Plastic, 2, 5–7, 9–10, 25, 31–34, 37–38, 43, 53, 61, 63, 70, 77, 79
Plow, plowing, 5, 21, 48, 50–51, 59–62
Pole, 1, 9, 69
Polychlorinated biphenyl (PCB), 38, 81
Polyethylene, 25
Polyvinylchloride (PVC), 25
Porcelain, 34
Pothead, 68–70
Premolded splice, 33–35
Pressure, 1, 4; *see also* Voltage
Primary, 4, 6, 10, 14–17, 19, 24–25, 31–34, 37, 39, 45, 57, 66, 75, 78–81, 83, 85–86

Rack, racking, 65, 67
Radar, 92
Radial circuit, system, 14, 82
Radio, 93
Reactance, 32
Recloser, 39
Relay, 16, 39, 86, 93, 95
Reliability, 6, 8–10, 13, 15, 18–19, 41
Review, 11–12, 22–23, 46–47, 70–71, 96–97
Right-of-way, 5–6
Riser, 39–40, 65, 69–70
Rubber, 4, 6, 25, 31, 44, 75, 77–78

Safety, 4, 19, 70, 81
Secondary, 4, 6, 17–20, 24–25, 32, 45, 57, 66, 69, 79–82
Secondary network, 17–18, 86; *see also* Low voltage network
Service, 4, 6, 19–20, 24, 62, 66, 69
Semi-stop joint, 29–30, 55, 77–78
Sewer, 21, 46, 54, 63

Sheath, 5–7, 24–26, 31–32, 44, 67–68, 70, 77
Short circuit, 19, 79, 86
Skin effect, 26
Solid type cable, 29, 52, 77–78
Spear, spiker, 79
Splice, splicing, 4–7, 21, 31–34, 46, 53, 55, 60, 62, 64–65, 67–68, 77, 79, 96; *see also* Joint
Steel, 5, 38, 43–44, 46, 53, 61, 82
Stop-joint, 29, 55, 77–78
Street lighting, 19, 24, 62
Study questions, 12, 23, 47, 71–72, 98
Substation, 3–5, 14, 17, 86
Sulfur hexafluoride, 27

Tank, 38, 80–82
Telegraph, 2
Telephone, 2, 7–9, 21
Test, 90–95
Tester, 79
"Thermal" sand, 52, 57
"Thumper," 92
Tile, 42, 53
Tracing current, 91
Tracking, 26–28
Transformer, 1, 4, 14–15, 17, 19–20, 24, 35–40, 42, 45, 51, 55, 62–63, 80–82, 84, 86, 93, 95
Transite, 42, 52
Transmission, 1, 4–5, 13–14, 24, 26, 29, 31, 41, 52, 55–56, 58, 66, 77, 86
Traveling wave, 92
Tree, tree trimming, 8
Trench, trenching, 48–49, 51–52, 57, 59, 61–63
Trough, 55–56
Trunk, 5; *see also* Conduit, duct
TV, 8

Underground, 1–2, 4–6, 8–11, 13–16, 18, 20–21, 24–25, 31–32, 36–37, 39–40, 42–43, 48, 52–53, 56, 58–59, 61–64, 67–69, 73, 80, 82, 86, 90, 96
URD, Underground residential distribution, 6

Vacuum, 37, 39, 55, 77–78
Varnished Cambric, 4, 6, 31, 44
Vault, 37, 40, 62–63, 75, 80–81
Ventilation, 55, 75–76
Vibratory plow, 50
Voltage, 1, 4–6, 10, 14, 17–19, 25–26, 31–32, 39–40, 52, 55, 66, 79, 82, 86, 90; *see also* Pressure
Voltage tester, 79
Voltmeter, 79, 86, 91

Water, 7, 21, 39, 46, 54, 57, 63, 75
Weatherhead, 69
Wheatstone bridge, 92